# THE TRAGEDY OF

# Julius Cæsar

EDITED BY

George Lyman Kittredge

*Revised by* Irving Ribner

*William Shakespeare*

# THE TRAGEDY OF

# Julius Cæsar

becoming.

a

wilson

JOHN WILEY & SONS

New York · London · Sydney · Toronto

# PREFACE

## The New Kittredge Shakespeares

The publication of George Lyman Kittredge's *Complete Works of Shakespeare* in 1936 was a landmark in Shakespeare scholarship. The teacher who for almost half a century had dominated and shaped the direction of Shakespearean study in America produced what was recognized widely as the finest edition of Shakespeare up to his time. In the preface to this edition Kittredge indicated his editorial principles; these allowed a paramount authority to the Folio of 1623 and countenanced few departures from it while, at the same time, refusing to "canonize the heedless type-setters of the Elizabethan printing house." Kittredge's work was marked by a judicious conservatism and a common sense rarely found in equal measure in earlier editors of Shakespeare. In the thirty-odd years which have gone by since the appearance of this monumental volume, however, considerable advances have been made in the establishment of Shakespeare's text, and our body of knowledge about the dates, sources, and general historical background of Shakespeare's plays has vastly increased. The present revision is designed to apply this new knowledge to Kittredge's work so that it may have as much value to the student and general reader of today as it had to those of thirty years ago.

Before his death Kittredge had issued in addition to *The Complete Works,* separate editions of sixteen of the plays, each copiously annotated. Some of the notes were unusually elaborate, but they interpreted Shakespeare's language with a fullness and precision attained by few other commentators, for Kittredge had few equals in his intimate knowledge of Elizabethan English. In freshly annotating the plays I have, accordingly, tried to use Kittredge's own notes as fully as space would permit. Where I have repeated his distinctive language or recorded his characteristic critical opinions, I have followed the note with the symbol [κ]; where Kittredge's definition of a term can be found in essentially the same words in other editions, I have not used the identifying symbol. Every annotator draws upon the full body of the notes of earlier editors, and to give credit for every note is impossible. Notes have been placed at page bottoms.

The brief introductions which Kittredge wrote for the plays have been replaced by new ones, for what seemed like indisputable fact some thirty years ago often appears today to be much more uncertain, and many new issues of which Kittredge was not aware have been raised in recent criticism. The new introductions seek to present what are now the generally agreed-upon basic facts about the plays and to give some indications of the directions which modern criticism has taken, although specific analyses of individual plays are avoided.

Such great authority attaches to Kittredge's text that it has not frequently — and never lightly — been departed from. Where changes have been made, they have usually involved the restoration of copy-text readings now generally accepted in place of the emendations of eighteenth- and nineteenth-century editors of which Kittredge, in spite of his extraordinary conservatism in this regard, sometimes too easily approved. Only rarely has an emendation been adopted in the present revision which was not also adopted by Kittredge. All departures from the copy-texts are indicated in the notes, emendations followed by the names of the editors by whom they were first proposed. Wherever Kittredge's text has been departed from for any reason, his reading is given in the notes. Modern spelling has in a few instances been substituted for Elizabethan forms which are mere spelling variations, but which Kittredge nevertheless retained. His punctuation has not been altered except in a few very rare instances.

The system of recording elisions and contractions which Kittredge explained in his introduction to *The Complete Works* has been retained, as has his method of preserving to the fullest the copy-text stage directions, with all additions to them enclosed within square brackets. Although modern editors recognize the vagueness of the place settings of Elizabethan plays and are reluctant to include the place designations so favoured by eighteenth- and nineteenth-century editors, much historical interest nevertheless attaches to these, and Kittredge's place designations accordingly have been retained between square brackets. Kittredge's attempt to retain the line numbering of the Globe text, which resulted in considerable irregularity in prose passages, has here been abandoned, and the lines of each play have been freshly numbered. Kittredge's act and scene divisions have been retained, as has his practice of surrounding by square brackets those divisions which are not in the copy-texts.

The *New Kittredge Shakespeares* include individual editions of each of the plays, the sonnets, and the minor poems, and a new edition of *The Complete Works* in a single volume. A comprehensive introduction to Shakespeare's life, times, and theatrical milieu is available both as a separate volume and as an introduction to *The Complete Works*.

IRVING RIBNER

# INTRODUCTION

## The Tragedy of Julius Cæsar

◇◇◇◇◇ *Julius Cæsar* was almost certainly written sometime in
◇◇◇◇◇ 1599, and staged in the autumn of that year. It is referred
to by John Weever in his *Mirror of Martyrs,* published in 1601,
though composed, as he tells us, two years before. A Swiss traveller
named Thomas Platter, who had visited England between Sep-
tember 18 and October 20, 1599, wrote upon his return home of a
play he had seen about the death of Julius Cæsar, at a theatre
with a thatched roof close to the Thames. That he was referring
to Shakespeare's play and that he saw it in the newly constructed
Globe Theatre on the Bankside may be accepted as certain. The
date is further confirmed by allusions in Ben Jonson's *Every Man
Out of His Humour,* itself acted in 1599. The play was extremely
popular in Shakespeare's day, as it has continued to be ever
since, but it was not printed before 1623 when it was included
in the Folio edition of Shakespeare's plays. This is an excellent
text, divided into acts, but without scene division, and it presents
relatively few textual problems. The present edition follows it
closely.

### SOURCES

The immediate source of *Julius Cæsar,* as of all Shakespeare's
Roman plays, was Sir Thomas North's *The Lives of the Noble
Grecians and Romanes,* first published in 1579 and again in 1595.
This translation of the *Parallel Lives* of Plutarch of Chaeronea is
itself a monument of Elizabethan prose, and it has been observed
that in the plays based upon North's *Plutarch,* Shakespeare follows his source more closely than in any others, sometimes varying

North's language only very slightly. Plutarch, a Greek who had lived from about A.D. 46 to 120, had spent much of his life in Rome, and in the most decadent period of the Roman empire he had looked back with nostalgia at what seemed to him a far greater past, writing his biographies so that the vices and virtues of earlier men might serve to guide those of his own time. North did not translate directly from Plutarch, however. He used instead the French version of Jacques Amyot, published in 1559, and since it is likely that Amyot himself had used a Latin version in addition to the Greek, Plutarch's account had undergone some changes in detail and in emphasis before it reached Shakespeare.

The story of the death of Cæsar was to Renaissance Englishmen perhaps the most widely known event in all Roman history, and Shakespeare doubtlessly read of it in other places besides Plutarch. As a schoolboy he probably read the letters written by Cicero to Atticus immediately after the assassination, as well as Cicero's Philippic oration on Mark Antony. It is likely that he knew Lucan's account of Cæsar in the *Pharsalia;* and it has recently been suggested that he read the translation of Appian's *Chronicles of the Roman Wars* published in 1578. He may have read Suetonius and Dion Cassius, and there were a great many Renaissance accounts of Cæsar which may have helped shape his view of the events of his play. Among the most significant of these is that of Michel de Montaigne, which he may have known in the French or in the English translation of John Florio. Although this was not published until after Shakespeare's play was written, Florio was translating Montaigne in the service of the Earl of Southampton, with whom there is strong reason to believe that Shakespeare had some connections, and he may well have seen the work in manuscript.

There was also a theatrical tradition which may have influenced him, for we have evidence of a good many earlier plays about Julius Cæsar. It has been argued, for instance, that he knew the anonymous play, *Cæsar's Revenge,* which must have been staged in the early 1590's, although it was not printed before 1606. There are also extant several Continental plays about Cæsar, the Latin *Julius Cæsar* of Marc-Antoine Muret published in 1553 and the French *Jules César* by Jacques Grévin, published in 1561. Although it is not likely that Shakespeare knew either of these plays, they are important as illustrating a dramatic tradition in which Cæsar was seen like Seneca's braggart Hercules, as one who by lawless pride and ambition had wrought his own destruction, suffering from the blindness with which the gods visit mere mortals who aspire to divinity.

It would be very convenient if we could distinguish a general Elizabethan way of looking at the murder of Julius Cæsar, as some scholars have sought to do. Cæsar's death, however, was one of the most widely written about and debated of all subjects in Shakespeare's day, and many conflicting attitudes towards it were current. Shakespeare drew much from North's *Plutarch,* but he was influenced also by a whole complex of sympathies and attitudes towards his subject, many hostile towards Cæsar and many sympathetic. Cæsar's fate and the ensuing events were used by some Elizabethan writers to illustrate how a great man carried away by pride and ambition could bring disaster to his own country.

## CONFLICTING VIEWS OF CÆSAR

In considering Shakespeare's *Julius Cæsar* we must remember the reverence and awe of ancient Rome which is so much a part of the Renaissance throughout Europe. Cæsar is always the greatest man the world has ever known and his murder a tragedy so cataclysmic as to be compared with the crucifixion of Christ. Indeed, Dante in his *Divine Comedy* had placed Brutus and Cassius in the very lowest circle of Hell, damned as the killers of their temporal lord, just as Judas is damned as the betrayer of his spiritual lord. Dante's is but one view, however, and it is one to be expected of him, the author of *De Monarchia*. For the champions of the monarchic ideal, Cæsar was a martyr and Brutus and Cassius his evil destroyers; for the champions of the Roman Republic, however, Brutus and Cassius were heroes. This division goes back to the time of Cæsar's death itself. To Lucan, Cicero, and other Roman republicans, Cæsar was a tyrant who had deserved destruction. To Plutarch he was a great and magnificent man corrupted by one single vice, the desire for kingship, which caused him to vitiate all he had achieved in life and to bring destruction to his country. Supporters of the Roman Empire like Livy and Suetonius condemned Brutus and Cassius in unequivocal terms. And this division of opinion continued into Shakespeare's time.

It is reflected also in modern criticism of Shakespeare's play. One critical view, reflected most notably by M. W. McCallam in *Shakespeare's Roman Plays and Their Background* (New York: Russell and Russell, Inc., 1964) and Sir Mark Hunter in *Transactions of the Royal Society of Literature* (1931), sees in the play a vindication of the monarchic principle: Cæsar the spirit of the monarchic ideal is destroyed by misguided men who bring ruin to their country and destruction to themselves, with Cæsar's spirit winning the final victory in the suicides of Brutus and Cassius. This view makes Brutus the hero of the play and sees in him a study of how a noble spirit can fall into tragic error through defect of reason. Another critical view, most notably reflected perhaps in John Dover Wilson's introduction to his New Cambridge edition of *Julius Cæsar* (1949), sees the play as about the threat of Cæsarism. Brutus in this view is correct in his estimate of Cæsar as a threat to human liberty, although he is not necessarily morally right in his decision to murder his friend, and the tragedy of the play is in the destruction of Brutus and the eventual triumph of a new Cæsarism embodied in Mark Antony because of the depravity of the Roman people. Still a third position, most notably expressed by Ernest Schanzer in *Problem Plays of Shakespeare* (New York: Schocken, 1963) sees *Julius Cæsar* as a problem play in the manner of *Measure for Measure* in which Shakespeare explores both points of view, exposing new facets of each, and leaves his audience finally in a state of ambivalence.

## THE TRAGEDY OF CÆSAR

There has been much controversy about who is to be regarded as the true hero of *Julius Cæsar*. Most critics have seen Brutus in this role, but others have argued for Cæsar, and still others have held that Rome is in effect the true hero of the play, for in the well-being of the state dramatic interest always resides. But no matter how we regard Julius Cæsar, it is evident that Shakespeare endows him with certain human weaknesses and that his own decision to go to the Senate House to be crowned is the immediate cause of his death. He is thus a tragic figure.

A common Renaissance view of Cæsar, as we have seen, was that of the great hero carried away by pride and ambition, refusing to acknowledge his own human limitations and aspiring to a position of godhood. This view is in Montaigne; it is in the Continental Cæsar plays by Muret and Grévin, and it appears also in a play called *Julius Cæsar* by William Alexander, Earl of Stirling, printed in 1607. Shakespeare's Cæsar, while not the Senecan overweening tyrant, nevertheless carries on something of this tradition. Throughout the play he denies his nature as a man with normal human limitations, claiming incapability of fear, imperviousness to flattery, and likening himself to the Northern star. But juxtaposed against every one of Cæsar's vaunting speeches is Shakespeare's reminder of Cæsar's physical infirmities, so that the boast of godhood appears as vain self-deception. Gods, Shakespeare constantly reminds us with a fine irony, do not suffer from deafness or fall into epileptic fits. Shakespeare's Cæsar, in spite of his many virtues, is guilty of pride in his refusal to acknowledge his own common humanity, and he is guilty of ambition in his aspiration to be king. These failings bring about his destruction, but the greatness of the man is such that his spirit survives and executes vengeance upon his murderers.

## THE TRAGEDY OF BRUTUS

Brutus is the most subtly drawn character of the play, and it seems that he interested Shakespeare more than any other. He has been censured by critics as pompous, self-righteous, incapable of the kind of human warmth which even Cassius expresses. Some critics have seen in him a portrait of a man so blinded by confidence in his own virtue and his own rational powers that he deceives himself and falls into tragic error. These critics would tend to see his error in his decision that Cæsar is a threat to Rome rather than Rome's great benefactor; his faulty logic leads him to embrace the cause of a futile republicanism rather than to support the principle of monarchy, the form of government thought to be most favoured by God. For his defect of reason he is destroyed.

It is possible, however, to agree with Brutus that Cæsar was a threat to Rome and still see him as a tragic figure who brings destruction upon himself and upon his country by his choice of an improper course of action. His moral error, in this view, is not his republicanism, but his decision to murder his friend, to commit a private crime in order to accomplish a public good, and thus to violate the Aristotelian principle that public virtue must rest upon private virtue, that a state can be well-governed only by good men, a principle which Shakespeare affirmed over and over again in his plays on English history.

Shakespeare's Brutus is actually a more attractive figure than his counterpart in Plutarch, for Shakespeare omits much which might have reflected unfavourably upon Brutus and perhaps obscured the dramatic issue which Granville-Barker in his *Prefaces to Shakespeare* (Princeton, N.J.: Princeton University Press, 1947) has called the problem of the "virtuous murderer." *Julius Cæsar* in the tragedy of Brutus poses the question of what may happen when a thoughtful man does evil so that greater good may result. Shakespeare omits, for instance, any suggestion that Brutus may have been the illegitimate son of Cæsar, as is suggested by Plutarch and other accounts as well. To have introduced the patricide theme, in spite of its great dramatic interest, might have sullied Brutus so much in the eyes of the audience as to obscure the real issues which were Shakespeare's concern. For perhaps the same reason he omits Plutarch's account of the rivalry for position between Brutus and Cassius, with Cæsar's constant favour towards Brutus in spite of the more valid claims of his rival.

### APPEARANCE AND REALITY

To do evil for the sake of good, Brutus is forced to blind himself to the true nature of his act. He attempts to clothe a brutal and bloody murder in the trappings of a ritual sacrifice. He would kill Cæsar's spirit without spilling his blood, but the irony is that this is impossible, and the hollowness of Brutus' self-deception is emphasized immediately after the murder when the conspirators, led by Brutus, do actually dip their arms up to the elbows in the blood of Cæsar. Brutus wishes to make moral and high-minded what is intrinsically an immoral act. It is for this reason that he denies the necessity for an oath — moral and honourable men do not need oaths — and he refuses to kill Antony as well as Cæsar. He would be a sacrificer and not a butcher.

Cassius, who proposes the oath and the death of Antony, recognizes, as Brutus does not, that in the act of killing Cæsar the conspirators have already forfeited their honour and morality, and that if the conspiracy is to be successfully concluded immoral means must be embraced. It is probably Cassius' chief function in the play to contrast in this manner with Brutus; he is the realist who from first to last sees all of the implications of the conspirators' actions, whereas Brutus is the idealist who deceives himself as to what he is really doing and continues to stand by honour and morality long after these have been forfeited. This is made clear by the great quarrel scene of the fourth act. Brutus would condemn Lucius Pella for taking bribes, for such a base act would stain the honour of all his party. Cassius recognizes that the taking of bribes is a small sin when compared to the murder of Cæsar, and that Lucius Pella is a soldier whose services are needed.

### CASSIUS AND ANTONY

In the various arguments between Cassius and Brutus, Cassius always gives in to his friend, although Cassius is always right, if not morally, certainly in terms of the practical ends of the conspiracy. It is necessary that he should do this in order to make clear the theme of Brutus' self-deception and to illustrate that a moral end cannot be attained by immoral means. But Cassius is a complex character. He can never be dismissed as a schemer or villain, as is sometimes done. He has an admiration for Brutus and a need for human affection which Shakespeare stresses strongly and which give a richness and humanity to his characterization.

Antony's relation to Cæsar is parallel to that of Cassius' to Brutus. It is Antony who tempts Cæsar to aspire to kingship by his offer of the crown, just as Cassius tempts Brutus into entering the conspiracy. Antony loves his friend, and Brutus underestimates the power of such friendship. After Cæsar's death, Antony becomes an embodiment of the spirit of Cæsar and thus the instrument of vengeance upon his murderers. The political force he represents, however, is even worse than that for which Cæsar had stood. This is made clear by his manipulation of the mob and by the cold-blooded proscription scene at the beginning of Act IV, in which the lives of kinsmen are brutally traded for one another. The pettiness and dissension which will mark the new rulers of Rome is made clear by Antony's treatment of Lepidus. If Cæsar had succumbed to pride and ambition, it had been at the end of a career of greatness and magnanimity; the Antony who will succeed Cæsar is marked by pettiness and political trickery. (He is not to be confused with the later Antony of *Antony and Cleopatra*, who is a character of an entirely different sort.)   In Antony's triumph at the end of the play we have a vision of what Brutus and Cassius have, in effect, succeeded in doing for their country.

# THE TRAGEDY OF

## Julius Cæsar

[DRAMATIS PERSONÆ

JULIUS CÆSAR.
OCTAVIUS CÆSAR,
MARCUS ANTONIUS,                    } *Triumvirs after the death*
M. ÆMILIUS LEPIDUS,                 *of* JULIUS CÆSAR.
CICERO,
PUBLIUS,                            } *Senators.*
POPILIUS LENA,
MARCUS BRUTUS,
CASSIUS,
CASCA,
TREBONIUS,
LIGARIUS,                           } *Conspirators against* JULIUS CÆSAR.
DECIUS BRUTUS,
METELLUS CIMBER,
CINNA,
FLAVIUS *and* MARULLUS, *Tribunes of the People.*
ARTEMIDORUS, *a Sophist.*
*A Soothsayer.*
CINNA, *a poet.*
*Another Poet.*
LUCILIUS,
TITINIUS,
MESSALA,                            } *friends to* BRUTUS *and* CASSIUS.
YOUNG CATO,
VOLUMNIUS,
VARRO,
CLITUS,
CLAUDIUS,                           } *servants to* BRUTUS.
STRATO,
LUCIUS,
DARDANIUS,
PINDARUS, *servant to* CASSIUS.
*A Servant to* CÆSAR; *to* ANTONY; *to* OCTAVIUS.

CALPHURNIA, *wife to* CÆSAR.
PORTIA, *wife to* BRUTUS.

*The Ghost of* CÆSAR.

*Senators, Citizens, Guards, Attendants, &c.*

SCENE. — *Rome; near Sardis; near Philippi.*]

# Act One

◇◇◇◇◇◇◇◇◇◇◇◇◇◇◇◇◇◇◇◇◇◇◇◇◇◇◇◇◇◇◇◇◇◇◇◇

SCENE I. [*Rome. A street.*]

*Enter* Flavius, Marullus, *and certain* Commoners *over
the stage.*

FLAV. Hence! home, you idle creatures, get you home!
Is this a holiday? What, know you not,
Being mechanical, you ought not walk
Upon a labouring day without the sign
Of your profession? Speak, what trade art thou? 5

CARP. Why, sir, a carpenter.

MAR. Where is thy leather apron and thy rule?
What dost thou with thy best apparel on?
You, sir, what trade are you?

COB. Truly, sir, in respect of a fine workman I am but, as you 10
would say, a cobbler.

MAR. But what trade art thou? Answer me directly.

COB. A trade, sir, that I hope I may use with a safe conscience,
which is indeed, sir, a mender of bad soles.

MAR. What trade, thou knave? Thou naughty knave, what
trade? 15

---

I.I. 3 *Being mechanical* having trades, belonging to the working class 4–5 *without
. . . profession* There is no record of laws, either Roman or Elizabethan, which re-
quired particular dress for workmen. 10 *in respect of* in comparison with. 11
*cobbler* (a) shoemaker (b) bungler. 12 *directly* plainly. 14 *soles* (a) shoe bottoms (b) souls (F¹: "soules"). 15 *Mar* CAPELL; F¹: "Fla." *naughty* worthless.

COB.   Nay, I beseech you, sir, be not out with me. Yet if you be
       out, sir, I can mend you.

MAR.   What mean'st thou by that? Mend me, thou saucy fellow?

COB.   Why, sir, cobble you.

FLAV.  Thou art a cobbler, art thou?                                  20

COB.   Truly, sir, all that I live by is with the awl. I meddle
       with no tradesman's matters nor women's matters, but
       with all. I am indeed, sir, a surgeon to old shoes. When
       they are in great danger, I recover them. As proper men
       as ever trod upon neat's leather have gone upon my      25
       handiwork.

FLAV.  But wherefore art not in thy shop to-day?
       Why dost thou lead these men about the streets?

COB.   Truly, sir, to wear out their shoes, to get myself into
       more work. But indeed, sir, we make holiday to see     30
       Cæsar and to rejoice in his triumph.

MAR.   Wherefore rejoice? What conquest brings he home?
       What tributaries follow him to Rome
       To grace in captive bonds his chariot wheels?
       You blocks, you stones, you worse than senseless things!  35
       O you hard hearts, you cruel men of Rome!
       Knew you not Pompey? Many a time and oft
       Have you climb'd up to walls and battlements,
       To tow'rs and windows, yea, to chimney tops,
       Your infants in your arms, and there have sat          40
       The livelong day, with patient expectation,
       To see great Pompey pass the streets of Rome.
       And when you saw his chariot but appear,
       Have you not made an universal shout,

---

16 *out* angry.    16–17 *be out* (a) out of temper (b) with holes in your shoes.    19
*cobble you* repair your shoes.    23 *all* The quibble on "awl" is a common one.
24 *recover* (a) repair (b) restore to health.    24–5 *As . . . leather* as good men as
ever worked on cowhide.    25 *gone* walked.    31 *triumph* victory procession. 32
*conquest . . . home* Cæsar's triumph was not for conquest of a foreign foe but
for victory in a civil war [K]. It was held in October, 45 B.C., following his defeat
of Pompey's sons at Munda in Spain.    33 *tributaries* captives.    34 *grace* do
honour to.    *captive bonds* chains.    35 *senseless* incapable of feeling.    46 *replication* echo.    47 *concave shores* overhanging banks.    49 *cull . . . holiday* select

That Tiber trembled underneath her banks                    45
To hear the replication of your sounds
Made in her concave shores?
And do you now put on your best attire?
And do you now cull out a holiday?
And do you now strew flowers in his way               50
That comes in triumph over Pompey's blood?
Be gone!
Run to your houses, fall upon your knees,
Pray to the gods to intermit the plague
That needs must light on this ingratitude.            55

FLAV.    Go, go, good countrymen, and for this fault
Assemble all the poor men of your sort;
Draw them to Tiber banks, and weep your tears
Into the channel, till the lowest stream
Do kiss the most exalted shores of all.               60

*Exeunt all the* Commoners.

See, whe'r their basest metal be not mov'd.
They vanish tongue-tied in their guiltiness.
Go you down that way towards the Capitol;
This way will I. Disrobe the images
If you do find them deck'd with ceremonies.           65

MAR.    May we do so?
You know it is the feast of Lupercal.

FLAV.    It is no matter. Let no images
Be hung with Cæsar's trophies. I'll about
And drive away the vulgar from the streets.           70
So do you too, where you perceive them thick.
These growing feathers pluck'd from Cæsar's wing

---

one out of the working days of the week and make a holiday of it [K].    51 *blood*
sons.    54 *intermit* postpone.    59-60 *till . . . all* so that the stream, even if it
is now at its lowest, may rise to the highest point it ever reaches, even in times
of flood [K].    61 *whe'r* whether (F¹: "where").    *metal* nature, disposition.    65
*ceremonies* triumphal ornaments.    67 *feast of Lupercal* celebrated in February in
honour of the Italian god Lupercus, worshipped as the protector of the flocks
against wolves and as a patron of agriculture [K].    69 *trophies* ornaments of
tribute.    *about* go about    70 *vulgar* common people.

Will make him fly an ordinary pitch,
Who else would soar above the view of men
And keep us all in servile fearfulness.           *Exeunt.*   75


◆◇◆◇◆◇◆◇◆◇◆◇◆◇◆


[SCENE II. *Rome. A public place.*]

[*Music.*] *Enter* Cæsar, Antony (*for the course*), Calphurnia, Portia, Decius, Cicero, Brutus, Cassius, Casca, [*a
   great crowd following, among them,*] *a* Soothsayer;
   *after them,* Marullus *and* Flavius.

CÆS.       Calphurnia.

CASCA.                     Peace, ho! Cæsar speaks.
                                      [*Music ceases.*]

CÆS.                                   Calphurnia.

CAL.       Here, my lord.

CÆS.       Stand you directly in Antonius' way
           When he doth run his course. Antonius.

ANT.       Cæsar, my lord?                                          5

CÆS.       Forget not in your speed, Antonius,
           To touch Calphurnia; for our elders say
           The barren, touched in this holy chase,
           Shake off their sterile curse.

ANT.                       I shall remember.
           When Cæsar says "Do this," it is perform'd.            10

CÆS.       Set on, and leave no ceremony out.       [*Music*]

SOOTH.     Cæsar!

---

73 *pitch* height (a falconry term meaning the highest point to which a hawk may
soar).    74 *above . . . men* out of the sight of men, as a god.
   I.II. 3 *Antonius'* POPE; F¹: "Antonio's" (and in lines 4 and 6).   4 *run his course*
in the footrace which was a traditional feature of the Lupercalia.   9 *sterile curse*
curse of sterility. It was believed that barren women would lose this curse if they
were struck by the leather thongs carried by the runners.   11 *Set on* move on.

| | |
|---|---|
| CÆS. | Ha! Who calls? |
| CASCA. | Bid every noise be still. Peace yet again! [*Music ceases.*] |
| CÆS. | Who is it in the press that calls on me?      15<br>I hear a tongue shriller than all the music<br>Cry "Cæsar!" Speak. Cæsar is turn'd to hear. |
| SOOTH. | Beware the ides of March. |
| CÆS. |                   What man is that? |
| BRU. | A soothsayer bids you beware the ides of March. |
| CÆS. | Set him before me; let me see his face.      20 |
| CASS. | Fellow, come from the throng; look upon Cæsar. |
| CÆS. | What say'st thou to me now? Speak once again. |
| SOOTH. | Beware the ides of March. |
| CÆS. | He is a dreamer. Let us leave him. Pass. |

*Sennet. Exeunt. Manent* Brutus *and* Cassius.

| | |
|---|---|
| CASS. | Will you go see the order of the course?      25 |
| BRU. | Not I. |
| CASS. | I pray you do. |
| BRU. | I am not gamesome. I do lack some part<br>Of that quick spirit that is in Antony.<br>Let me not hinder, Cassius, your desires.      30<br>I'll leave you. |
| CASS. | Brutus, I do observe you now of late;<br>I have not from your eyes that gentleness<br>And show of love as I was wont to have.<br>You bear too stubborn and too strange a hand      35<br>Over your friend that loves you. |
| BRU. |                   Cassius, |

---

15 *press* crowd.   24 *Sennet* flourish of trumpets.   25 *order of the course* pro-
ceedings at the race.   28 *gamesome* frivolous.   29 *quick spirit* lively disposition.
34 *show* appearance.  *love* friendship.  *wont* accustomed.   35–6 *You bear . . .
you* you treat your friend too roughly and too much like a stranger. The figure
is from riding or driving a horse [K] 35 *stubborn* harsh.  *strange* estranged.

Be not deceiv'd. If I have veil'd my look,
I turn the trouble of my countenance
Merely upon myself. Vexed I am
Of late with passions of some difference,                     40
Conceptions only proper to myself,
Which give some soil, perhaps, to my behaviours;
But let not therefore my good friends be griev'd
(Among which number, Cassius, be you one)
Nor construe any further my neglect                           45
Than that poor Brutus, with himself at war,
Forgets the shows of love to other men.

CASS.    Then, Brutus, I have much mistook your passion;
By means whereof this breast of mine hath buried
Thoughts of great value, worthy cogitations.                 50
Tell me, good Brutus, can you see your face?

BRU.     No, Cassius; for the eye sees not itself
But by reflection, by some other things.

CASS.    'Tis just.
And it is very much lamented, Brutus,                         55
That you have no such mirrors as will turn
Your hidden worthiness into your eye,
That you might see your shadow. I have heard
Where many of the best respect in Rome
(Except immortal Cæsar), speaking of Brutus                   60
And groaning underneath this age's yoke,
Have wish'd that noble Brutus had his eyes.

BRU.     Into what dangers would you lead me, Cassius,
That you would have me seek into myself
For that which is not in me?                                  65

---

37–9 *If . . . myself* if my looks have been less open and friendly, the troubled expression of my face is altogether due to personal matters (not to unfriendliness toward you) [K].   40 *passions . . . difference* conflicting emotions.   41 *Conceptions . . . myself* thoughts which concern only me.   42 *soil* blemish.   43 *griev'd* offended.   45 *construe any further* read any other meaning into.   47 *shows* outward signs.   48 *passion* feelings.   49 *By means . . . buried* because of which I have kept to myself.   52–3 *eye . . . reflection* the eye can see itself only by reflection, as in a mirror.   54 *just* true.   56 *turn* reflect.   57 *hidden worthiness* noble qualities of which you seem unaware.   58 *shadow* image in a mirror.   59 *best respect* highest regard.   60 *immortal Cæsar* In this sudden and bitter parenthesis Cassius allows his hatred of Caesar to show itself for a moment [K].   62

CASS.    Therefore, good Brutus, be prepar'd to hear;
And since you know you cannot see yourself
So well as by reflection, I, your glass,
Will modestly discover to yourself
That of yourself which you yet know not of.      70
And be not jealous on me, gentle Brutus.
Were I a common laughter, or did use
To stale with ordinary oaths my love
To every new protester; if you know
That I do fawn on men and hug them hard,      75
And after scandal them; or if you know
That I profess myself in banqueting
To all the rout, then hold me dangerous.

                             *Flourish and shout.*

BRU.    What means this shouting? I do fear the people
Choose Cæsar for their king.

CASS.                         Ay, do you fear it?      80
Then must I think you would not have it so.

BRU.    I would not, Cassius; yet I love him well.
But wherefore do you hold me here so long?
What is it that you would impart to me?
If it be aught toward the general good,      85
Set honour in one eye and death i' th' other,
And I will look on both indifferently;
For let the gods so speed me as I love
The name of honour more than I fear death.

CASS.    I know that virtue to be in you, Brutus,      90

---

had his eyes could see; were not blind to his own merits [K].    69 *modestly* without exaggeration.    69 *discover* make known.    71 *jealous on* suspicious of.    72 *laughter* laughing-stock (F¹; ROWE. K: "laugher").    73 *stale . . . love* cheapen my friendship.    74 *protester* declarer of friendship.    76 *scandal* slander.    78 *rout* common crowd.    *hold* consider.    83 *hold* detain.    85 *general good* welfare of the state.    86–7 *Set . . . indifferently* place death and honour before me and I will judge between them without bias, not permitting fear of death to affect my judgment of the supreme value of honour [K].    88 *speed me* make me prosper.    90 *that virtue* that manly virtue of preferring honour to everything else — even to life [K].

As well as I do know your outward favour.
Well, honour is the subject of my story.
I cannot tell what you and other men
Think of this life; but for my single self,
I had as lief not be as live to be      95
In awe of such a thing as I myself.
I was born free as Cæsar; so were you.
We both have fed as well, and we can both
Endure the winter's cold as well as he.
For once, upon a raw and gusty day,      100
The troubled Tiber chafing with her shores,
Cæsar said to me, "Dar'st thou, Cassius, now
Leap in with me into this angry flood
And swim to yonder point?" Upon the word,
Accoutred as I was, I plunged in      105
And bade him follow. So indeed he did.
The torrent roar'd, and we did buffet it
With lusty sinews, throwing it aside
And stemming it with hearts of controversy.
But ere we could arrive the point propos'd,      110
Cæsar cried, "Help me, Cassius, or I sink!"
I, as Æneas, our great ancestor,
Did from the flames of Troy upon his shoulder
The old Anchises bear, so from the waves of Tiber
Did I the tired Cæsar. And this man      115
Is now become a god, and Cassius is
A wretched creature and must bend his body
If Cæsar carelessly but nod on him.
He had a fever when he was in Spain,
And when the fit was on him, I did mark      120
How he did shake. 'Tis true, this god did shake.

---

91 *favour* face.    96 *as I myself* He is emphasizing that Cæsar is just another mortal, not God's special agent on earth, as Tudor political theory defined a King. 101 *chafing with* raging against.    105 *Accoutred* dressed in armour.    109 *of controversy* full of rivalry.    112 *Æneas* legendary founder of Rome.    117 *bend* bow.    120 *fit* chill.    122 *coward lips* The speaker's scorn finds expression, naturally enough in a grotesque play on words. The lips are said to have "abandoned their colour(s)" like cowardly soldiers [K].    123 *bend* glance.    124 *his* its. 129 *temper* physical constitution.    130 *get . . . world* Cæsar has outstripped the whole world in the race for power [K].    131 *palm* victor's prize.    136 *Colossus* a giant statue of Apollo believed to have spanned the harbour at Rhodes.

His coward lips did from their colour fly,
And that same eye whose bend doth awe the world
Did lose his lustre. I did hear him groan.
Ay, and that tongue of his that bade the Romans                125
Mark him and write his speeches in their books,
Alas, it cried, "Give me some drink, Titinius,"
As a sick girl! Ye gods, it doth amaze me
A man of such a feeble temper should
So get the start of the majestic world                         130
And bear the palm alone.

*Shout. Flourish.*

BRU. Another general shout?
  I do believe that these applauses are
  For some new honours that are heap'd on Cæsar.

CASS. Why, man, he doth bestride the narrow world        135
  Like a Colossus, and we petty men
  Walk under his huge legs and peep about
  To find ourselves dishonourable graves.
  Men at some time are masters of their fates.
  The fault, dear Brutus, is not in our stars,          140
  But in ourselves, that we are underlings.
  "Brutus," and "Cæsar." What should be in that "Cæsar"?
  Why should that name be sounded more than yours?
  Write them together: yours is as fair a name.
  Sound them: it doth become the mouth as well.          145
  Weigh them: it is as heavy. Conjure with 'em:
  "Brutus" will start a spirit as soon as "Cæsar."
  Now in the names of all the gods at once,
  Upon what meat doth this our Cæsar feed

---

137-8 *peep . . . graves* Cæsar's supremacy has closed every career of honourable ambition. There is nothing for us to seek except our own graves; and even those will be dishonourable, for they will not be the graves of freemen [K].  140 *our stars* the stars that rule our lives. Cassius means that submission is a matter in which every one may choose for himself. No man is forced by fate to be Cæsar's slave [K]. In limiting the power of the stars over human life, Cassius is stating a view contrary to that of most Elizabethans.  143 *sounded more* be more celebrated in men's talk [K].  145 *sound* pronounce.  146 *Conjure* raise spirits.  147 *start* raise up a spirit.

That he is grown so great? Age, thou art sham'd!     150
Rome, thou hast lost the breed of noble bloods!
When went there by an age since the great Flood
But it was fam'd with more than with one man?
When could they say (till now) that talk'd of Rome
That her wide walks encompass'd but one man?     155
Now is it Rome indeed, and room enough,
When there is in it but one only man!
O, you and I have heard our fathers say
There was a Brutus once that would have brook'd
Th' eternal devil to keep his state in Rome     160
As easily as a king.

BRU.     That you do love me I am nothing jealous.
What you would work me to, I have some aim.
How I have thought of this, and of these times,
I shall recount hereafter. For this present,     165
I would not (so with love I might entreat you)
Be any further mov'd. What you have said
I will consider; what you have to say
I will with patience hear, and find a time
Both meet to hear and answer such high things.     170
Till then, my noble friend, chew upon this:
Brutus had rather be a villager
Than to repute himself a son of Rome
Under these hard conditions as this time
Is like to lay upon us.

CASS.                    I am glad     175
That my weak words have struck but thus much show
Of fire from Brutus.

*Enter* Cæsar *and his* Train.

BRU.     The games are done, and Cæsar is returning.

---

151 *lost . . . bloods* your nobles are all degenerate.     152 *great Flood* that of
Deucalion, the classical analogue of Noah.     153 *fam'd with* made famous by.
155 *walks* F¹; ROWE, K: "walls."     156 *room* pronounced to rhyme with "Rome."
159 *Brutus once* Lucius Junius Brutus, who had helped drive the Tarquins from
Rome.     159–61 *that would . . . king* that would have been as ready to give
Rome over to the rule of the devil forever as to allow a king to set up his throne
there [K].     162 *nothing jealous* not at all doubtful.     163 *work* persuade.

| | |
|---|---|
| CASS. | As they pass by, pluck Casca by the sleeve, |
| | And he will (after his sour fashion) tell you                      180 |
| | What hath proceeded worthy note to-day. |
| BRU. | I will do so. But look you, Cassius! |
| | The angry spot doth glow on Cæsar's brow, |
| | And all the rest look like a chidden train. |
| | Calphurnia's cheek is pale, and Cicero                            185 |
| | Looks with such ferret and such fiery eyes |
| | As we have seen him in the Capitol, |
| | Being cross'd in conference by some senators. |
| CASS. | Casca will tell us what the matter is. |
| CÆS. | Antonius.                                                        190 |
| ANT. | Cæsar? |
| CÆS. | Let me have men about me that are fat, |
| | Sleek-headed men, and such as sleep a-nights. |
| | Yond Cassius has a lean and hungry look. |
| | He thinks too much. Such men are dangerous.                      195 |
| ANT. | Fear him not, Cæsar; he's not dangerous. |
| | He is a noble Roman, and well given. |
| CÆS. | Would he were fatter! But I fear him not. |
| | Yet if my name were liable to fear, |
| | I do not know the man I should avoid                             200 |
| | So soon as that spare Cassius. He reads much, |
| | He is a great observer, and he looks |
| | Quite through the deeds of men. He loves no plays |
| | As thou dost, Antony; he hears no music. |
| | Seldom he smiles, and smiles in such a sort                       205 |
| | As if he mock'd himself and scorn'd his spirit |
| | That could be mov'd to smile at anything. |
| | Such men as he be never at heart's ease |

---

*aim* guess.   165 *this present* now.   166 *so . . . you* if I may request it as a friend.   167 *mov'd* persuaded.   170 *high* serious.   174 *as* which.   175 *like* likely.   178 *games* the footrace.   181 *proceeded* taken place.   186 *ferret* blood-shot (from angry excitement). The ferret has small red eyes.   188 *cross'd* op-posed. *conference* debate.   190 *Antonius* POPE; F¹: "Antonio."   197 *given* disposed.   205 *sort* way.

Whiles they behold a greater than themselves,
And therefore are they very dangerous.                    210
I rather tell thee what is to be fear'd
Than what I fear; for always I am Cæsar.
Come on my right hand, for this ear is deaf,
And tell me truly what thou think'st of him.

> *Sennet. Exeunt* Cæsar *and his* Train.
> [*Manet* Casca.]

CASCA.  You pull'd me by the cloak. Would you speak with me?  215

BRU.    Ay, Casca. Tell us what hath chanc'd to-day
        That Cæsar looks so sad.

CASCA.  Why, you were with him, were you not?

BRU.    I should not then ask Casca what had chanc'd.

CASCA.  Why, there was a crown offer'd him; and being offer'd  220
        him, he put it by with the back of his hand thus; and
        then the people fell a-shouting.

BRU.    What was the second noise for?

CASCA.  Why, for that too.

CASS.   They shouted thrice. What was the last cry for?         225

CASCA.  Why, for that too.

BRU.    Was the crown offer'd him thrice?

CASCA.  Ay, marry, was't! and he put it by thrice, every time
        gentler than other; and at every putting-by mine honest
        neighbours shouted.                                    230

CASS.   Who offer'd him the crown?

CASCA.  Why, Antony.

BRU.    Tell us the manner of it, gentle Casca.

---

209 *Whiles* so long as.   213 *ear is deaf* This graphic touch is Shakespeare's own.
There is no ancient authority for Cæsar's deafness [K]. Coming as it does immediately after Cæsar's claim to divinity, it underscores with irony that he is merely
a man after all, suffering from the most human of infirmities.   217 *sad* serious.
228 *marry* to be sure.   229 *honest* worthy.   235 *mere foolery* pure, downright
pretense.   236–7 *one of these coronets* A coronet ("little crown") is a crown of an
inferior sort appropriate not to kings but to dukes. "These" expresses contempt.

CASCA. I can as well be hang'd as tell the manner of it. It was mere foolery; I did not mark it. I saw Mark Antony offer 235 him a crown — yet 'twas not a crown neither, 'twas one of these coronets — and, as I told you, he put it by once; but for all that, to my thinking, he would fain have had it. Then he offered it to him again; then he put it by again; but to my thinking, he was very loath to lay his 240 fingers off it. And then he offered it the third time. He put it the third time by; and still as he refus'd it, the rabblement hooted, and clapp'd their chopt hands, and threw up their sweaty nightcaps, and uttered such a deal of stinking breath because Cæsar refus'd the crown that 245 it had, almost, chok'd Cæsar; for he swounded and fell down at it. And for mine own part, I durst not laugh, for fear of opening my lips and receiving the bad air.

CASS. But soft, I pray you. What, did Cæsar swound?

CASCA. He fell down in the market place and foam'd at mouth 250 and was speechless.

BRU. 'Tis very like. He hath the falling sickness.

CASS. No, Cæsar hath it not; but you, and I, And honest Casca, we have the falling sickness.

CASCA. I know not what you mean by that, but I am sure Cæsar 255 fell down. If the tag-rag people did not clap him and hiss him, according as he pleas'd and displeas'd them, as they use to do the players in the theatre, I am no true man.

BRU. What said he when he came unto himself? 260

CASCA. Marry, before he fell down, when he perceiv'd the com-mon herd was glad he refus'd the crown, he pluck'd me

---

What Antony really offered to Cæsar was a wreath of gold which bore some re-semblance to a crown [K].    238 *fain* gladly.    242 *still as* every time that.    243 *hooted* shouted in approval (F[1]: "howted").    246 *swounded* swooned. This inci-dent is of Shakespeare's own invention, but he got the hint from Plutarch [K]. 249 *soft* slowly.    252 *like* likely.    *falling sickness* epilepsy, to which Cæsar had been subject from his youth [K].    256 *tag-rag* low and ragged.    258 *use* are accustomed.    *true* honest.

ope his doublet and offer'd them his throat to cut. An I
had been a man of any occupation, if I would not have
taken him at a word I would I might go to hell among   265
the rogues. And so he fell. When he came to himself
again, he said, if he had done or said anything amiss, he
desir'd their worships to think it was his infirmity. Three
or four wenches where I stood cried "Alas, good soul!"
and forgave him with all their hearts. But there's no   270
heed to be taken of them. If Cæsar had stabb'd their
mothers, they would have done no less.

BRU.   And after that, he came thus sad away?

CASCA.   Ay.

CASS.   Did Cicero say anything?   275

CASCA.   Ay, he spoke Greek.

CASS.   To what effect?

CASCA.   Nay, an I tell you that, I'll ne'er look you i' th' face
again. But those that understood him smil'd at one an-
ther and shook their heads; but for mine own part, it   280
was Greek to me. I could tell you more news too. Marullus and Flavius, for pulling scarfs off Cæsar's images, are
put to silence. Fare you well. There was more foolery
yet, if I could remember it.

CASS.   Will you sup with me to-night, Casca?   285

CASCA.   No, I am promis'd forth.

CASS.   Will you dine with me to-morrow?

CASCA.   Ay, if I be alive, and your mind hold, and your dinner
worth the eating.

---

263 *doublet* a kind of close-fitting coat. Shakespeare's Romans are clothed in
Elizabethan garb [K]. There is some possibility, however, that they wore togas;
the matter is uncertain. *An* if.   264 *man . . . occupation* (a) mechanic or
tradesman (since Cæsar had offered his throat to such Plebeians to be cut) (b)
man of action.   265 *taken . . . word* taken him at his word instantly [K].   268
*infirmity* epilepsy.   281 *Greek* unintelligible.   283 *put to silence* suppressed;
forbidden to take any part in public affairs [K].   288 *your mind hold* you still
desire my company.   292 *blunt* dull, slow-witted.   293 *quick mettle* of a lively

| | |
|---|---|
| CASS. | Good. I will expect you. 290 |
| CASCA. | Do so. Farewell both. *Exit.* |
| BRU. | What a blunt fellow is this grown to be! |
| | He was quick mettle when he went to school. |
| CASS. | So is he now in execution |
| | Of any bold or noble enterprise, 295 |
| | However he puts on this tardy form. |
| | This rudeness is a sauce to his good wit, |
| | Which gives men stomach to disgest his words |
| | With better appetite. |
| BRU. | And so it is. For this time I will leave you. 300 |
| | To-morrow, if you please to speak with me, |
| | I will come home to you; or if you will, |
| | Come home to me, and I will wait for you. |
| CASS. | I will do so. Till then, think of the world. *Exit* Brutus. |
| | Well, Brutus, thou art noble; yet I see 305 |
| | Thy honourable mettle may be wrought |
| | From that it is dispos'd. Therefore it is meet |
| | That noble minds keep ever with their likes; |
| | For who so firm that cannot be seduc'd? |
| | Cæsar doth bear me hard; but he loves Brutus. 310 |
| | If I were Brutus now and he were Cassius, |
| | He should not humour me. I will this night, |
| | In several hands, in at his windows throw, |
| | As if they came from several citizens, |
| | Writings, all tending to the great opinion 315 |
| | That Rome holds of his name; wherein obscurely |
| | Cæsar's ambition shall be glanced at. |
| | And after this let Cæsar seat him sure, |
| | For we will shake him, or worse days endure. *Exit.* |

---

nature.   296 *tardy form* pose of sluggishness.   298 *stomach* appetite.   *disgest* digest.   302 *come home to* visit.   306–7 *wrought . . . dispos'd* so worked upon as to acquire a quality quite different from its native disposition [K].   310 *bear me hard* looks upon me with disfavour [K].   312 *humour* cajole; win over by the art of flattery [K].   313 *hands* handwritings.   315 *tending . . . opinion* stressing the great respect.   317 *ambition* lawless greed for power [K].   *glanced* hinted.   318 *seat him sure* establish himself securely.

◇◇◇◇◇◇◇◇◇◇◇◇◇◇◇

[SCENE III. *Rome. A street.*]

*Thunder and lightning. Enter, [from opposite sides,]*
*Casca, [with his sword drawn,] and* Cicero.

CIC.       Good even, Casca. Brought you Cæsar home?
           Why are you breathless? and why stare you so?

CASCA.     Are not you mov'd when all the sway of earth
           Shakes like a thing unfirm? O Cicero,
           I have seen tempests when the scolding winds                    5
           Have riv'd the knotty oaks, and I have seen
           Th' ambitious ocean swell and rage and foam
           To be exalted with the threat'ning clouds;
           But never till to-night, never till now,
           Did I go through a tempest dropping fire.                       10
           Either there is a civil strife in heaven,
           Or else the world, too saucy with the gods,
           Incenses them to send destruction.

CIC.       Why, saw you any thing more wonderful?

CASCA.     A common slave (you know him well by sight)                     15
           Held up his left hand, which did flame and burn
           Like twenty torches join'd; and yet his hand,
           Not sensible of fire, remain'd unscorch'd.
           Besides (I ha' not since put up my sword),
           Against the Capitol I met a lion,                               20
           Who glaz'd upon me, and went surly by
           Without annoying me. And there were drawn
           Upon a heap a hundred ghastly women,
           Transformed with their fear, who swore they saw
           Men, all in fire, walk up and down the streets.                 25

---

I.III. 1 *Brought* escorted.    3 *all the sway of earth* the whole sovereign power of
earth; all this mighty earth, supreme in its stability — the one fixed and stable
thing in the universe according to the old system of astronomy [K].    6 *riv'd* split.
12 *saucy* insolent.    14 *wonderful* awe-inspiring. 18 *sensible of* capable of feeling.
20 *Against* next to.    21 *glaz'd* stared fixedly (F¹; ROWE, K: "glar'd").    22–3 *drawn
. . . heap* huddled together.    26 *bird of night* owl, a traditionally ill-omened
creature.    28 *prodigies* supernatural phenomena, such as were believed to occur

And yesterday the bird of night did sit
Even at noonday upon the market place,
Hooting and shrieking. When these prodigies
Do so conjointly meet, let not men say
"These are their reasons — they are natural,"          30
For I believe they are portentous things
Unto the climate that they point upon.

CIC.     Indeed it is a strange-disposed time.
But men may construe things after their fashion,
Clean from the purpose of the things themselves.          35
Comes Cæsar to the Capitol to-morrow?

CASCA.   He doth; for he did bid Antonius
Send word to you he would be there to-morrow.

CIC.     Good night then, Casca. This disturbed sky
Is not to walk in.

CASCA.                   Farewell, Cicero.          *Exit* Cicero.   40

*Enter* Cassius.

CASS.    Who's there?

CASCA.              A Roman.

CASS.                         Casca, by your voice.

CASCA.   Your ear is good. Cassius, what night is this!

CASS.    A very pleasing night to honest men.

CASCA.   Who ever knew the heavens menace so?

CASS.    Those that have known the earth so full of faults.          45
For my part, I have walk'd about the streets,
Submitting me unto the perilous night,
And, thus unbraced, Casca, as you see,
Have bar'd my bosom to the thunder-stone;

---

before cataclysmic events on earth.    29 *conjointly meet* coincide in time and place
and agree in their apparent meaning [K].    32 *climate* region, country.    33
*strange-disposed* abnormal, extraordinary.    34 *construe . . . fashion* interpret in
their own way, in accordance with their own fancy [K].    35 *Clean . . . themselves*
in a way utterly opposed to their real meaning [K].    49 *thunder-stone* thunder-
bolt.

And when the cross blue lightning seem'd to open          50
The breast of heaven, I did present myself
Even in the aim and very flash of it.

CASCA.  But wherefore did you so much tempt the heavens?
It is the part of men to fear and tremble
When the most mighty gods by tokens send          55
Such dreadful heralds to astonish us.

CASS.  You are dull, Casca, and those sparks of life
That should be in a Roman you do want,
Or else you use not. You look pale, and gaze,
And put on fear, and cast yourself in wonder,          60
To see the strange impatience of the heavens;
But if you would consider the true cause —
Why all these fires, why all these gliding ghosts,
Why birds and beasts, from quality and kind;
Why old men fool and children calculate;          65
Why all these things change from their ordinance,
Their natures, and preformed faculties,
To monstrous quality — why, you shall find
That heaven hath infus'd them with these spirits
To make them instruments of fear and warning          70
Unto some monstrous state.
Now could I, Casca, name to thee a man
Most like this dreadful night
That thunders, lightens, opens graves, and roars
As doth the lion in the Capitol;          75
A man no mightier than thyself or me
In personal action, yet prodigious grown
And fearful, as these strange eruptions are.

---

50 *cross* zigzag.    53 *tempt* try experiments with, take liberties with [K].    56 *astonish* frighten and fill with awe.    58 *want* lack.    60 *cast . . . wonder* throw yourself, or plunge, into a state of unreasoning amazement [K].    61 *impatience* violence.    64 *Why birds . . . kind* why birds and beasts are, or conduct themselves, contrary to their characteristic quality — their nature [K].    65 *Why . . . calculate* why old men, who are naturally wise, act and talk like fools, and children, who are naturally foolish, show prophetic wisdom [K].    66 *ordinance* appointed and regular behaviour.    67 *preformed faculties* foreordained or established powers and functions [K].    68 *monstrous quality* behaviour contrary to nature.    71 *monstrous state* some government or commonwealth that is in an abnormal condition [K].    72 *a man* Cassius declares that this man is quite as ab-

| | | |
|---|---|---|
| CASCA. | 'Tis Cæsar that you mean. Is it not, Cassius? | |
| CASS. | Let it be who it is. For Romans now | 80 |
| | Have thews and limbs like to their ancestors; | |
| | But woe the while! our fathers' minds are dead, | |
| | And we are govern'd with our mothers' spirits; | |
| | Our yoke and sufferance show us womanish. | |
| CASCA. | Indeed, they say the senators to-morrow | 85 |
| | Mean to establish Cæsar as a king, | |
| | And he shall wear his crown by sea and land | |
| | In every place save here in Italy. | |
| CASS. | I know where I will wear this dagger then; | |
| | Cassius from bondage will deliver Cassius. | 90 |
| | Therein, ye gods, you make the weak most strong; | |
| | Therein, ye gods, you tyrants do defeat. | |
| | Nor stony tower, nor walls of beaten brass, | |
| | Nor airless dungeon, nor strong links of iron, | |
| | Can be retentive to the strength of spirit; | 95 |
| | But life, being weary of these worldly bars, | |
| | Never lacks power to dismiss itself. | |
| | If I know this, know all the world besides, | |
| | That part of tyranny that I do bear | |
| | I can shake off at pleasure.   *Thunder still.* | |
| CASCA. | So can I. | 100 |
| | So every bondman in his own hand bears | |
| | The power to cancel his captivity. | |
| CASS. | And why should Cæsar be a tyrant then? | |
| | Poor man! I know he would not be a wolf | |
| | But that he sees the Romans are but sheep; | 105 |

normal as the phenomena just described, and that his existence is as ominous to the Roman world as these fearful prodigies which have so terrified Casca [K].   **77** *prodigious* unnatural, threatening.   **78** *fearful* giving cause for fear.   *eruptions* outbursts of the violent forces of nature [K].   **81** *thews* sinews.   **82** *woe the while* woe be to the time.   **83** *mothers' spirits* the fearful dispositions of women.   **84** *yoke and sufferance* not merely the fact that we wear the yoke, but that we wear it patiently [K].   **92** *defeat* thwart.   **95** *Can . . . spirit* can hold in, or confine, a strong nature. Bolts and bars can imprison the man's body, but not the man himself [K].   **97** *dismiss* liberate.   **102** *cancel* nullify a bond, a legal term suggested by "bondman" in the preceding line.

He were no lion, were not Romans hinds.
Those that with haste will make a mighty fire
Begin it with weak straws. What trash is Rome,
What rubbish and what offal, when it serves
For the base matter to illuminate                               110
So vile a thing as Cæsar! But, O grief,
Where hast thou led me? I, perhaps, speak this
Before a willing bondman. Then I know
My answer must be made. But I am arm'd,
And dangers are to me indifferent.                              115

CASCA.  You speak to Casca, and to such a man
That is no fleering telltale. Hold, my hand.
Be factious for redress of all these griefs,
And I will set this foot of mine as far
As who goes farthest.

CASS.                              There's a bargain made.      120
Now know you, Casca, I have mov'd already
Some certain of the noblest-minded Romans
To undergo with me an enterprise
Of honourable-dangerous consequence;
And I do know, by this they stay for me                         125
In Pompey's Porch; for now, this fearful night,
There is no stir or walking in the streets,
And the complexion of the element
In favour's like the work we have in hand,
Most bloody, fiery, and most terrible.                          130

*Enter* Cinna.

CASCA.  Stand close awhile, for here comes one in haste.

CASS.  'Tis Cinna. I do know him by his gait.

---

106 *hinds* (a) female deer, i.e. cowards (b) rustics or servants.    111 *vile* worthless.
114 *My answer . . . made* I shall have to answer [to Cæsar] for my words. If
Casca is a willing bondman, he will act the informer [K].    *arm'd* capable of
committing suicide.    117 *fleering* flattering, smiling obsequiously.    118 *Be
factious* form a faction or party.    *griefs* grievances.    123 *undergo* undertake.    124
*consequence* not "result," but simply "the future." What follows in the course of
this enterprise will be both honourable and dangerous [K].    125 *this* this time.
126 *Pompey's Porch* Pompey's portico or colonnade, attached to Pompey's Theatre
in the Campus Martius. The "curia" or Senate House, also erected by Pompey, was

He is a friend. Cinna, where haste you so?

CIN.    To find out you. Who's that? Metellus Cimber?

CASS.    No, it is Casca, one incorporate                    135
To our attempts. Am I not stay'd for, Cinna?

CIN.    I am glad on't. What a fearful night is this!
There's two or three of us have seen strange sights.

CASS.    Am I not stay'd for? Tell me.

CIN.                            Yes, you are.
O Cassius, if you could                              140
But win the noble Brutus to our party —

CASS.    Be you content. Good Cinna, take this paper
And look you lay it in the prætor's chair,
Where Brutus may but find it. And throw this
In at his window. Set this up with wax             145
Upon old Brutus' statue. All this done,
Repair to Pompey's Porch, where you shall find us.
Is Decius Brutus and Trebonius there?

CIN.    All but Metellus Cimber, and he's gone
To seek you at your house. Well, I will hie          150
And so bestow these papers as you bade me.

CASS.    That done, repair to Pompey's Theatre.    *Exit* Cinna.
Come, Casca, you and I will yet ere day
See Brutus at his house. Three parts of him
Is ours already, and the man entire                  155
Upon the next encounter yields him ours.

CASCA.    O, he sits high in all the people's hearts;
And that which would appear offence in us,
His countenance, like richest alchemy,

---

near. In the "curia Pompei" was held the meeting of the Senate at which Cæsar was
assassinated. Shakespeare has shifted the scene of the murder to the Capitol.    128
*complexion of the element* condition of the sky.    129 *In favour's like* resembles in
appearance or quality (Q of 1691; F¹: "Is, Fauors, like").    131 *close* concealed.
135 *incorporate* united with us.    136 *stay'd for* expected.    137 *on't* of it.    143
*prætor* magistrate.    146 *old Brutus* Brutus's illustrious ancestor.    151 *bestow*
deposit.    156 *encounter* (a) meeting (b) assault.    159 *countenance* approval, support.    159 *alchemy* the science which aimed to transmute base metals into gold,
studied earnestly in Shakespeare's time and well into the eighteenth century.

Will change to virtue and to worthiness.                    160

CASS.  Him and his worth and our great need of him
       You have right well conceited. Let us go,
       For it is after midnight; and ere day
       We will awake him and be sure of him.        *Exeunt.*

160 *worthiness* honourable conduct.    162 *conceited* conceived, understood.  *go* to
the rendezvous at Pompey's Porch. They intend to call on Brutus after the general
meeting of the conspirators [K].

# Act Two

◇◇◇◇◇◇◇◇◇◇◇◇◇◇◇◇◇◇◇◇◇◇◇◇◇◇◇◇◇◇◇◇◇◇◇◇◇◇◇◇◇◇◇◇◇◇◇◇◇◇◇◇

[SCENE I. *Rome.*]

*Enter* Brutus *in his orchard.*

BRU.    What, Lucius, ho!
I cannot by the progress of the stars
Give guess how near to day. Lucius, I say!
I would it were my fault to sleep so soundly.
When, Lucius, when? Awake, I say! What, Lucius!        5

*Enter* Lucius.

LUC.    Call'd you, my lord?

BRU.    Get me a taper in my study, Lucius.
When it is lighted, come and call me here.

LUC.    I will, my lord.                                    *Exit.*

BRU.    It must be by his death; and for my part,          10
I know no personal cause to spurn at him,
But for the general. He would be crown'd.
How that might change his nature, there's the question.
It is the bright day that brings forth the adder,
And that craves wary walking. Crown him — that!          15
And then I grant we put a sting in him
That at his will he may do danger with.

---

II.I. In the interval between the acts Cassius has taken Casca to the meeting of the conspirators at Pompey's Theatre. Cinna has joined them there after disposing of the papers given him by Cassius. Scene 1 opens a little before dawn on the ides (the 15th) of March. The place is Brutus's orchard — the garden attached to his house. Brutus has just risen after a sleepless night [K].    2 *progress* movement. 7 *taper* candle.    11 *spurn* kick.    12 *general* public at large.    15 *craves* requires. 17 *danger* harm.

Th' abuse of greatness is, when it disjoins
Remorse from power. And to speak truth of Cæsar,
I have not known when his affections sway'd          20
More than his reason. But 'tis a common proof
That lowliness is young ambition's ladder,
Whereto the climber-upward turns his face;
But when he once attains the upmost round,
He then unto the ladder turns his back,              25
Looks in the clouds, scorning the base degrees
By which he did ascend. So Cæsar may.
Then lest he may, prevent. And since the quarrel
Will bear no colour for the thing he is,
Fashion it thus: that what he is, augmented,         30
Would run to these and these extremities;
And therefore think him as a serpent's egg,
Which, hatch'd, would as his kind grow mischievous,
And kill him in the shell.

Enter Lucius.

LUC.    The taper burneth in your closet, sir.       35
Searching the window for a flint, I found
This paper, thus seal'd up; and I am sure
It did not lie there when I went to bed.

Gives him the letter.

BRU.    Get you to bed again; it is not day.
Is not to-morrow, boy, the ides of March?            40

LUC.    I know not, sir.

BRU.    Look in the calendar and bring me word.

LUC.    I will, sir.                          Exit.

---

18–19 *Th'abuse . . . power* the misuse of authority comes ordinarily from the
fact that absolute rulers forget what mercy [remorse] means [K].    20 *affections
sway'd* passions and impulses ruled him.    21 *common proof* a matter of common
experience; and therefore to be feared in Cæsar's case [K].    22 *lowliness* humility.
24 *upmost round* top rung of the ladder.    26 *base degrees* (a) lower rungs (b)
lesser positions.    28 *prevent* forestall.    28 *quarrel* the cause of complaint; the
case against Cæsar as a man [K].    29 *bear no colour* carry no appearance of justice
[K].    30 *Fashion it thus* state the case as follows.    30 *augmented* with the addition of a crown.    31 *extremities* kinds of tyranny.    33 *as his kind* like the rest
of his species.    *mischievous* harmful.    35 *taper* candle.    *closet* study.    40 *ides*

BRU.    The exhalations, whizzing in the air,
Give so much light that I may read by them.    45

*Opens the letter and reads.*

"Brutus, thou sleep'st. Awake, and see thyself!
Shall Rome, &c. Speak, strike, redress!"

"Brutus, thou sleep'st. Awake!"
Such instigations have been often dropp'd
Where I have took them up.    50
"Shall Rome, &c." Thus must I piece it out:
Shall Rome stand under one man's awe? What, Rome?
My ancestors did from the streets of Rome
The Tarquin drive when he was call'd a king.
"Speak, strike, redress!" Am I entreated    55
To speak and strike? O Rome, I make thee promise,
If the redress will follow, thou receivest
Thy full petition at the hand of Brutus!

*Enter* Lucius.

LUC.    Sir, March is wasted fifteen days.    *Knock within.*

BRU.    'Tis good. Go to the gate; somebody knocks.    60

[*Exit.* Lucius.]

Since Cassius first did whet me against Cæsar,
I have not slept.
Between the acting of a dreadful thing
And the first motion, all the interim is
Like a phantasma or a hideous dream.    65
The genius and the mortal instruments
Are then in council, and the state of man,
Like to a little kingdom, suffers then

---

THEOBALD; F¹: "first."    44 *exhalations* meteors, formerly ascribed to the combustion of gases exhaled from the heavenly bodies. The meteors in question were amongst the omens which were said to have portended the death of Cæsar [K]. 64 *first motion* initial proposal or suggestion.    65 *phantasma* nightmare.    66–7 *genius . . . council* the immortal or spiritual aspect of man (genius) and the physical parts of man (mortal instruments), with their human passions, are in conflict with one another.    67 *state of man* the man himself conceived as a state or commonwealth, or, as we read in the next line, as a kingdom in miniature. The comparison of a man to a state or a state to a man (as in the phrase "body politic") is very common [K].

The nature of an insurrection.

*Enter* Lucius.

LUC. Sir, 'tis your brother Cassius at the door,    70
Who doth desire to see you.

BRU.                         Is he alone?

LUC. No, sir, there are moe with him.

BRU.                            Do you know them?

LUC. No, sir. Their hats are pluck'd about their ears
And half their faces buried in their cloaks,
That by no means I may discover them    75
By any mark of favour.

BRU.                   Let 'em enter.     [*Exit* Lucius.]
They are the faction. O conspiracy,
Sham'st thou to show thy dang'rous brow by night,
When evils are most free? O, then by day
Where wilt thou find a cavern dark enough    80
To mask thy monstrous visage? Seek none, conspiracy.
Hide it in smiles and affability!
For if thou path, thy native semblance on,
Not Erebus itself were dim enough
To hide thee from prevention.    85

*Enter the Conspirators,* Cassius, Casca,
Decius, Cinna, Metellus [Cimber], *and*
Trebonius.

CASS. I think we are too bold upon your rest.
Good morrow, Brutus. Do we trouble you?

BRU. I have been up this hour, awake all night.
Know I these men that come along with you?

CASS. Yes, every man of them; and no man here    90

---

70 *brother* actually brother-in-law, since Cassius, according to North's PLUTARCH, had married Junia, Brutus's sister.   72 *moe* more.   75 *discover* recognize.   76 *favour* feature, appearance.   77 *faction* party.   79 *evils . . . free* It was commonly believed that evil spirits walked at night.   83 *path . . . on* walk in your normal manner or guise. The line has been much emended, but the F[1] reading makes perfect sense.   84 *Erebus* the dark region through which spirits must pass from earth to Hades.   85 *prevention* hindrance by anticipation, forestalling

But honours you; and every one doth wish
You had but that opinion of yourself
Which every noble Roman bears of you.
This is Trebonius.

BRU.                    He is welcome hither.

CASS.    This, Decius Brutus.

BRU.                    He is welcome too.    95

CASS.    This, Casca; this, Cinna; and this, Metellus Cimber.

BRU.    They are all welcome.
What watchful cares do interpose themselves
Betwixt your eyes and night?

CASS.    Shall I entreat a word?    *They whisper.*  100

DEC.    Here lies the east. Doth not the day break here?

CASCA.    No.

CIN.    O, pardon, sir, it doth; and yon grey lines
That fret the clouds are messengers of day.

CASCA.    You shall confess that you are both deceiv'd.    105
Here, as I point my sword, the sun arises,
Which is a great way growing on the south,
Weighing the youthful season of the year.
Some two months hence, up higher toward the north
He first presents his fire; and the high east    110
Stands as the Capitol, directly here.

BRU.    Give me your hands all over, one by one.

CASS.    And let us swear our resolution.

BRU.    No, not an oath. If not the face of men,
The sufferance of our souls, the time's abuse —    115
If these be motives weak, break off betimes,

---

[K].    86 *upon your rest* in interfering with your sleep.    104 *fret* interlace.    107
*growing on* tending toward [K].    108 *Weighing* considering.    111 *as the Capitol*
as the Capitol does, the Capitol is due east from this point [K].    114 *face of
men* the sad and anxious looks of our fellow-citizens [K].    115 *sufferance* suffering.  *time's abuse* present abuses.    116 *motives* incentives to action.  *betimes* in
good season.

And every man hence to his idle bed.
So let high-sighted tyranny range on
Till each man drop by lottery. But if these
(As I am sure they do) bear fire enough                    120
To kindle cowards and to steel with valour
The melting spirits of women, then, countrymen,
What need we any spur but our own cause
To prick us to redress? what other bond
Than secret Romans that have spoke the word               125
And will not palter? and what other oath
Than honesty to honesty engag'd
That this shall be, or we will fall for it?
Swear priests and cowards and men cautelous,
Old feeble carrions and such suffering souls              130
That welcome wrongs; unto bad causes swear
Such creatures as men doubt; but do not stain
The even virtue of our enterprise,
Nor th' insuppressive mettle of our spirits,
To think that or our cause or our performance             135
Did need an oath; when every drop of blood
That every Roman bears, and nobly bears,
Is guilty of a several bastardly
If he do break the smallest particle
Of any promise that hath pass'd from him.                 140

CASS.     But what of Cicero? Shall we sound him?
I think he will stand very strong with us.

CASCA.    Let us not leave him out.

CIN.                          No, by no means.

MET.      O, let us have him! for his silver hairs
Will purchase us a good opinion                           145

---

118 *high-sighted* haughty, arrogant [K]. The term is from falconry: tyranny, like
a hawk, being capable of seeing from great height.     119 *Till . . . lottery* until
every man worthy of the name has fallen a victim to the capricious enmity of the
tyrant [K].     122 *melting spirits* feeble, yielding temperaments [K].     124 *prick* in-
cite.     125 *secret Romans* Romans engaged in secret affairs.     126 *palter* be deceitful.     127 *honesty* personal honour. *engag'd* pledged.     129 *cautelous* cautious,
overcautious, suspicious. The word sometimes means "crafty" or "wily," which
would also fit the sense here [K].     130 *carrions* men so weak as to be almost dead.

And buy men's voices to commend our deeds.
It shall be said his judgment rul'd our hands.
Our youths and wildness shall no whit appear,
But all be buried in his gravity.

BRU.    O, name him not! Let us not break with him;    150
For he will never follow anything
That other men begin.

CASS.                        Then leave him out.

CASCA.    Indeed he is not fit.

DEC.    Shall no man else be touch'd but only Cæsar?

CASS.    Decius, well urg'd. I think it is not meet    155
Mark Antony, so well belov'd of Cæsar,
Should outlive Cæsar. We shall find of him
A shrewd contriver; and you know, his means,
If he improve them, may well stretch so far
As to annoy us all; which to prevent,    160
Let Antony and Cæsar fall together.

BRU.    Our course will seem too bloody, Caius Cassius,
To cut the head off and then hack the limbs,
Like wrath in death and envy afterwards;
For Antony is but a limb of Cæsar.    165
Let us be sacrificers, but not butchers, Caius.
We all stand up against the spirit of Cæsar,
And in the spirit of men there is no blood.
O that we then could come by Cæsar's spirit
And not dismember Cæsar! But, alas,    170
Cæsar must bleed for it! And, gentle friends,
Let's kill him boldly, but not wrathfully;

---

133 *even virtue* uniform and consistent excellence [K].    134 *insuppressive mettle* indomitable temper.    138 *guilty . . . bastardly* shows that he is not of true Roman blood.    148 *no whit* not at all.    149 *gravity* stability and sobriety of character. The word implies also the "weight" or "authority" which belongs to such a character [K].    150 *break with* confide in.    155 *urg'd* suggested.    156 *of* by.    157 *of him* on his part, in him.    158 *shrewd* troublesome, pestilent, dangerous [K].    159 *improve* use, turn to advantage.    160 *annoy* injure.    *prevent* forestall.    164 *envy* malice.    171 *gentle* honourable, noble.

Let's carve him as a dish fit for the gods,
Not hew him as a carcass fit for hounds.
And let our hearts, as subtle masters do,                    175
Stir up their servants to an act of rage
And after seem to chide 'em. This shall make
Our purpose necessary, and not envious;
Which so appearing to the common eyes,
We shall be call'd purgers, not murderers.                   180
And for Mark Antony, think not of him;
For he can do no more than Cæsar's arm
When Cæsar's head is off.

CASS.                         Yet I fear him;
For in the ingrafted love he bears to Cæsar —

BRU.    Alas, good Cassius, do not think of him!              185
If he love Cæsar, all that he can do
Is to himself — take thought, and die for Cæsar.
And that were much he should; for he is given
To sports, to wildness, and much company.

TREB.   There is no fear in him. Let him not die;            190
For he will live, and laugh at this hereafter.

*Clock strikes.*

BRU.    Peace! Count the clock.

CASS.                         The clock hath stricken three.

TREB.   'Tis time to part.

CASS.                         But it is doubtful yet
Whether Cæsar will come forth to-day or no;
For he is superstitious grown of late,                       195

---

176 *servants* In this simile the "hearts" correspond to the masters and the "hands"
to the servants. They are not to be angry in their hearts, though their hands per-
form a necessary "act of rage" [K].    177 *make* cause to appear.    178 *envious*
malicious.    180 *purgers* healers.    184 *ingrafted* so deeply implanted as to be a
part of himself [K].    187 *take thought, and die* fall into melancholy and pine
away [K].    188 *were much* is not likely that.    190 *fear* cause for fear (on our
part).    196 *main opinion . . . once* contrary to the strong opinion which he once
held. Cæsar, who professed the Epicurean philosophy, was convinced of the futility of signs and omens [K].    197 *fantasy* fancy; hence, in this passage, signs and
omens that affect the imagination, imaginary terrors [K].    198 *apparent* manifest,

Quite from the main opinion he held once
Of fantasy, of dreams, and ceremonies.
It may be these apparent prodigies,
The unaccustom'd terror of this night,
And the persuasion of his augurers　　　　　　200
May hold him from the Capitol to-day.

DEC.　Never fear that. If he be so resolv'd,
I can o'ersway him; for he loves to hear
That unicorns may be betray'd with trees
And bears with glasses, elephants with holes,　　205
Lions with toils, and men with flatterers;
But when I tell him he hates flatterers,
He says he does, being then most flattered.
Let me work;
For I can give his humour the true bent　　　　210
And I will bring him to the Capitol.

CASS.　Nay, we will all of us be there to fetch him.

BRU.　By the eighth hour. Is that the uttermost?

CIN.　Be that the uttermost, and fail not then.

MET.　Caius Ligarius doth bear Cæsar hard,　　　　215
Who rated him for speaking well of Pompey.
I wonder none of you have thought of him.

BRU.　Now, good Metellus, go along by him.
He loves me well, and I have given him reasons.
Send him but hither, and I'll fashion him.　　　220

CASS.　The morning comes upon's. We'll leave you, Brutus.
And, friends, disperse yourselves; but all remember

---

striking.　*prodigies* unnatural phenomena.　200 *augurers* augurs, prophets.
203 *o'ersway* overcome by persuasion.　204 *unicorns . . . trees* The story was that
the hunter dodges behind a tree when the unicorn charges, so that the creature's
horn sticks fast in the trunk [K].　205 *glasses* mirrors, which attract the bear's
gaze and enable the hunter to approach him unperceived [K].　205 *holes* pit-
falls.　206 *toils* nets or snares.　210 *humour* feelings, disposition.　*bent* direction, inclination.　212 *fetch* escort.　213 *eighth* F⁴; F¹ "eight." *uttermost* latest.
215 *doth . . . hard* has a grudge against Cæsar.　216 *rated* berated.　218 *go
along by him* call on him as you pass his house.　220 *fashion* mould (to our will).

What you have said and show yourselves true Romans.

BRU.   Good gentlemen, look fresh and merrily.
       Let not our looks put on our purposes,                    225
       But bear it as our Roman actors do,
       With untir'd spirits and formal constancy.
       And so good morrow to you every one.

                                  *Exeunt. Manet* Brutus.

       Boy! Lucius! Fast asleep? It is no matter.
       Enjoy the honey-heavy dew of slumber.                     230
       Thou hast no figures nor no fantasies
       Which busy care draws in the brains of men;
       Therefore thou sleep'st so sound.

                          *Enter* Portia.

POR.                            Brutus, my lord!

BRU.   Portia! What mean you? Wherefore rise you now?
       It is not for your health thus to commit                  235
       Your weak condition to the raw cold morning.

POR.   Nor for yours neither. Y' have ungently, Brutus,
       Stole from my bed. And yesternight at supper
       You suddenly arose and walk'd about,
       Musing and sighing with your arms across;                 240
       And when I ask'd you what the matter was,
       You star'd upon me with ungentle looks.
       I urg'd you further; then you scratch'd your head
       And too impatiently stamp'd with your foot.
       Yet I insisted; yet you answer'd not,                     245
       But with an angry wafture of your hand
       Gave sign for me to leave you. So I did,
       Fearing to strengthen that impatience
       Which seem'd too much enkindled, and withal
       Hoping it was but an effect of humour,                    250

---

225 *put . . . purposes* reveal our intentions.    226–7 *bear it . . . constancy* conduct the affair, as our actors play their parts, with unflagging energy and unruffled self-possession [K].    230 *dew* Sleep is often called "dew" because it is conceived as falling gently and imperceptibly from above [K].    231 *figures* anxious ideas. 237 *ungently* discourteously.    240 *across* folded, in the position of one absorbed in thought.    246 *wafture* wave (ROWE; F¹: "wafter").    249 *withal* at the same time, besides.    250 *effect of humour* symptom of some passing mood (due to accidental

Which sometime hath his hour with every man.
It will not let you eat nor talk nor sleep,
And could it work so much upon your shape
As it hath much prevail'd on your condition,
I should not know you Brutus. Dear my lord,                  255
Make me acquainted with your cause of grief.

BRU.  I am not well in health, and that is all.

POR.  Brutus is wise and, were he not in health,
He would embrace the means to come by it.

BRU.  Why, so I do. Good Portia, go to bed.                  260

POR.  Is Brutus sick, and is it physical
To walk unbraced and suck up the humours
Of the dank morning? What, is Brutus sick,
And will he steal out of his wholesome bed
To dare the vile contagion of the night,                     265
And tempt the rheumy and unpurged air,
To add unto his sickness? No, my Brutus.
You have some sick offence within your mind,
Which by the right and virtue of my place
I ought to know of; and upon my knees                        270
I charm you, by my once commended beauty,
By all your vows of love, and that great vow
Which did incorporate and make us one,
That you unfold to me, yourself, your half,
Why you are heavy — and what men to-night                    275
Have had resort to you; for here have been
Some six or seven, who did hide their faces
Even from darkness.

BRU.                          Kneel not, gentle Portia.

POR.  I should not need if you were gentle Brutus.

---

disturbance in the physical temperament) [k].    253 *shape* outward appearance.
254 *condition* disposition.    259 *come by* obtain.    262 *unbraced* with the doublet
unbuttoned or unlaced.  *humours* damp mists.    266 *tempt* risk.  *rheumy* moist,
dank, causing colds.    268 *sick offence* sickness that troubles you [k].    271 *charm*
solemnly beg.    273 *incorporate* make us one body.    274 *unfold* disclose.    275
*heavy* sad.  *to-night* this night just past.

Within the bond of marriage, tell me, Brutus,                   280
Is it excepted I should know no secrets
That appertain to you? Am I yourself
But, as it were, in sort or limitation?
To keep with you at meals, comfort your bed,
And talk to you sometimes? Dwell I but in the suburbs   285
Of your good pleasure? If it be no more,
Portia is Brutus' harlot, not his wife.

BRU.    You are my true and honourable wife,
As dear to me as are the ruddy drops
That visit my sad heart.                                      290

POR.    If this were true, then should I know this secret.
I grant I am a woman; but withal
A woman that Lord Brutus took to wife.
I grant I am a woman; but withal
A woman well-reputed, Cato's daughter.                    295
Think you I am no stronger than my sex,
Being so father'd and so husbanded?
Tell me your counsels; I will not disclose 'em.
I have made strong proof of my constancy,
Giving myself a voluntary wound                           300
Here, in the thigh. Can I bear that with patience,
And not my husband's secrets?

BRU.                              O ye gods,
Render me worthy of this noble wife!         *Knock.*
Hark, hark! One knocks. Portia, go in awhile,
And by-and-by thy bosom shall partake                     305
The secrets of my heart.
All my engagements I will construe to thee,
All the charactery of my sad brows.

---

283 *in sort or limitation* after a fashion or in a restricted sense [K].    284 *keep*
remain.    285 *suburbs* the resort of disreputable persons.    289–90 *ruddy drops*
. . . *heart* blood.    295 *Cato's daughter* Portia's father was Marcus Porcius Cato,
a Stoic philosopher known for his rigid morality. He had been a follower of
Pompey and committed suicide — in violation of his Stoic creed
— after Pompey's defeat by Cæsar.    298 *counsels* secrets.
tude.    301 *patience* calmness, self-control.    307–8 *construe . . . brows* fully ex-
plain the meaning (charactery, literally, handwriting) of the expression of my sad

Leave me with haste.                    *Exit* Portia.
                        Lucius, who's that knocks?

                    *Enter* Lucius *and* [Caius] Ligarius.

LUC.    Here is a sick man that would speak with you.        310

BRU.    Caius Ligarius, that Metellus spake of.
        Boy, stand aside. Caius Ligarius, how?

CAIUS.  Vouchsafe good-morrow from a feeble tongue.

BRU.    O, what a time have you chose out, brave Caius,
        To wear a kerchief! Would you were not sick!        315

CAIUS.  I am not sick if Brutus have in hand
        Any exploit worthy the name of honour.

BRU.    Such an exploit have I in hand, Ligarius,
        Had you a healthful ear to hear of it.

CAIUS.  By all the gods that Romans bow before,             320
        I here discard my sickness! [*Throws off his kerchief.*] Soul
            of Rome!
        Brave son, deriv'd from honourable loins!
        Thou like an exorcist hast conjur'd up
        My mortified spirit. Now bid me run,
        And I will strive with things impossible;           325
        Yea, get the better of them. What's to do?

BRU.    A piece of work that will make sick men whole.

CAIUS.  But are not some whole that we must make sick?

BRU.    That must we also. What it is, my Caius,
        I shall unfold to thee as we are going               330
        To whom it must be done.

CAIUS.                      Set on your foot,
        And with a heart new-fir'd I follow you,

---

face.   310 *a sick man* Lucius knows by the kerchief that Ligarius is sick [K].   313
*Vouchsafe* deign to accept.   314 *brave* noble.   315 *kerchief* a linen head-cloth
regularly worn indoors by women. If a man fell sick, his first act was to wrap his
head up in a kerchief for warmth and protection against draughts [K].   319
*healthful* (a) physically sound (b) receptive.   323 *exorcist* one who calls up spirits.
324 *mortified* paralyzed.   330 *unfold* disclose.   331 *To whom* to the house of
him to whom. *Set on* advance.

To do I know not what; but it sufficeth
That Brutus leads me on.                    *Thunder.*

BRU.                         Follow me then.    *Exeunt.*

◇◇◇◇◇◇◇◇◇◇◇◇◇◇◇

[SCENE II. *Rome.* Cæsar's *house.*]

*Thunder and lightning. Enter* Julius Cæsar, *in his nightgown.*

CÆS.    Nor heaven nor earth have been at peace to-night.
Thrice hath Calphurnia in her sleep cried out
"Help, ho! They murder Cæsar!" Who's within?

*Enter a* Servant.

SERV.    My lord?

CÆS.    Go bid the priests do present sacrifice,          5
And bring me their opinions of success.

SERV.    I will, my lord.                         *Exit.*

*Enter* Calphurnia.

CAL.    What mean you, Cæsar? Think you to walk forth?
You shall not stir out of your house to-day.

CÆS.    Cæsar shall forth. The things that threaten'd me    10
Ne'er look'd but on my back. When they shall see
The face of Cæsar, they are vanished.

CAL.    Cæsar, I never stood on ceremonies,
Yet now they fright me. There is one within,
Besides the things that we have heard and seen,    15
Recounts most horrid sights seen by the watch.

---

II.II. s.d. *nightgown* What is meant is a warm garment, something like a modern
dressing gown, which it was customary to put on immediately after rising from bed
and before dressing [K]. 5 *present* immediate.   6 *success* outcome.   10 *Cæsar
shall forth* Throughout the scene Cæsar's language and bearing are marked by
such pomposity that critics have accused Shakespeare of either misapprehending
or misrepresenting him [K]. The strutting, braggart Cæsar, however, was a well-

A lioness hath whelped in the streets,
And graves have yawn'd and yielded up their dead.
Fierce fiery warriors fight upon the clouds
In ranks and squadrons and right form of war,                20
Which drizzled blood upon the Capitol.
The noise of battle hurtled in the air,
Horses did neigh, and dying men did groan,
And ghosts did shriek and squeal about the streets.
O Cæsar, these things are beyond all use,                    25
And I do fear them!

CÆS.                     What can be avoided
Whose end is purpos'd by the mighty gods?
Yet Cæsar shall go forth; for these predictions
Are to the world in general as to Cæsar.

CAL.     When beggars die there are no comets seen;          30
The heavens themselves blaze forth the death of princes.

CÆS.     Cowards die many times before their deaths;
The valiant never taste of death but once.
Of all the wonders that I yet have heard,
It seems to me most strange that men should fear,            35
Seeing that death, a necessary end,
Will come when it will come.

               *Enter a* Servant.

                    What say the augurers?

SERV.     They would not have you to stir forth to-day.
Plucking the entrails of an offering forth,
They could not find a heart within the beast.                40

CÆS.     The gods do this in shame of cowardice.
Cæsar should be a beast without a heart
If he should stay at home to-day for fear.
No, Cæsar shall not. Danger knows full well

---

established tradition.     13 *stood on ceremonies* gave heed to omens.     19 *fight* F¹;
ᴋ: "fought."     20 *right form* regular order.     22 *hurtled* clashed together.     23 *did
neigh* F²; F¹: "do neigh."     25 *beyond all use* contrary to ordinary experience.
26–7 *What . . . gods* what event whose fulfillment the gods have purposed can be
avoided by mortals [ᴋ].     37 *augurers* augurs, soothsayers.     42 *should* would certainly.

That Cæsar is more dangerous than he.    45
We are two lions litter'd in one day,
And I the elder and more terrible,
And Cæsar shall go forth.

CAL.                        Alas, my lord!
Your wisdom is consum'd in confidence.
Do not go forth to-day. Call it my fear    50
That keeps you in the house and not your own.
We'll send Mark Antony to the Senate House,
And he shall say you are not well to-day.
Let me upon my knee prevail in this.

CÆS.    Mark Antony shall say I am not well,    55
And for thy humour I will stay at home.

*Enter* Decius.

Here's Decius Brutus; he shall tell them so.

DEC.    Cæsar, all hail! Good morrow, worthy Cæsar!
I come to fetch you to the Senate House.

CÆS.    And you are come in very happy time    60
To bear my greeting to the senators
And tell them that I will not come to-day.
Cannot, is false; and that I dare not, falser:
I will not come to-day. Tell them so, Decius.

CAL.    Say he is sick.

CÆS.                        Shall Cæsar send a lie?    65
Have I in conquest stretch'd mine arm so far
To be afeard to tell greybeards the truth?
Decius, go tell them Cæsar will not come.

DEC.    Most mighty Cæsar, let me know some cause,
Lest I be laugh'd at when I tell them so.    70

---

49 *consum'd in confidence* destroyed by overconfidence.    56 *humour* whim, caprice.
58 *worthy* noble.    59 *fetch* escort.    60 *happy time* opportune moment.    73 *satisfaction* information.    75 *stays* detains.    76 *to-night* last night.    78 *lusty* merry.
80 *apply for* consider to be.    88–9 *great men . . . cognizance* great men shall be
eager for a share in the fresh lifeblood of prosperity which your rule will infuse
into the veins of Rome; and they shall throng about you for that share as eagerly

CÆS. The cause is in my will: I will not come.
   That is enough to satisfy the Senate;
   But for your private satisfaction,
   Because I love you, I will let you know.
   Calphurnia here, my wife, stays me at home.  75
   She dreamt to-night she saw my statuë,
   Which, like a fountain with an hundred spouts,
   Did run pure blood; and many lusty Romans
   Came smiling and did bathe their hands in it.
   And these does she apply for warnings and portents 80
   And evils imminent, and on her knee
   Hath begg'd that I will stay at home to-day.

DEC. This dream is all amiss interpreted;
   It was a vision fair and fortunate.
   Your statue spouting blood in many pipes,  85
   In which so many smiling Romans bath'd,
   Signifies that from you great Rome shall suck
   Reviving blood, and that great men shall press
   For tinctures, stains, relics, and cognizance.
   This by Calphurnia's dream is signified.  90

CÆS. And this way have you well expounded it.

DEC. I have, when you have heard what I can say;
   And know it now. The Senate have concluded
   To give this day a crown to mighty Cæsar.
   If you shall send them word you will not come, 95
   Their minds may change. Besides, it were a mock
   Apt to be render'd, for some one to say
   "Break up the Senate till another time,
   When Cæsar's wife shall meet with better dreams."
   If Cæsar hide himself, shall they not whisper 100
   "Lo, Cæsar is afraid"?

---

as devotees press forward to dip their handkerchiefs in the blood of a martyr [K].
89 *tinctures* handkerchiefs dipped in the blood of martyrs, supposed to have heal-
ing powers (synonymous with "stains"). 89 *cognizance* a heraldic badge, worn
to show that one belongs to the household of some great noble [K]. 97 *Apt*
ready. *render'd* spoken in reply.

Pardon me, Cæsar; for my dear dear love
To your proceeding bids me tell you this,
And reason to my love is liable.

CÆS.   How foolish do your fears seem now, Calphurnia!    105
I am ashamed I did yield to them.
Give me my robe, for I will go.

> *Enter* Brutus, Ligarius, Metellus,
> Casca, Trebonius, Cinna, *and* Publius.

And look where Publius is come to fetch me.

PUB.   Good morrow, Cæsar.

CÆS.                         Welcome, Publius.
What, Brutus, are you stirr'd so early too?    110
Good morrow, Casca. Caius Ligarius,
Cæsar was ne'er so much your enemy
As that same ague which hath made you lean.
What is't o'clock?

BRU.                         Cæsar, 'tis strucken eight.

CÆS.   I thank you for your pains and courtesy.    115

> *Enter* Antony.

See! Antony, that revels long a-nights,
Is notwithstanding up. Good morrow, Antony.

ANT.   So to most noble Cæsar.

CÆS.                         Bid them prepare within.
I am to blame to be thus waited for.
Now, Cinna. Now, Metellus. What, Trebonius;    120
I have an hour's talk in store for you;

---

102 *my dear dear love* The hypocrisy of this speech goes beyond anything that we
can pardon even in the most patriotic conspirator. Shakespeare intends to make
Decius hateful to us, and at the same time to show how blinded Cæsar is by self-
confidence [K].    103 *proceeding* advancement.    104 *reason . . . liable* propriety
is subordinate to my devotion. My devotion to your interests is such that I must
speak frankly, even at the risk of using improper freedom [K].    112 *your enemy*
Ligarius, who had taken part in the Civil War on Pompey's side, had recently

   Remember that you call on me to-day;
   Be near me, that I may remember you.

TREB. Cæsar, I will. [*Aside*] And so near will I be
   That your best friends shall wish I had been further.  125

CÆS. Good friends, go in and taste some wine with me,
   And we (like friends) will straightway go together.

BRU. [*aside*] That every like is not the same, O Cæsar,
   The heart of Brutus erns to think upon.  *Exeunt.* 129

◇◇◇◇◇◇◇◇◇◇◇◇◇◇

  [SCENE III. *Rome. A street near the Capitol.*]

  *Enter* Artemidorus, [*reading a paper*].

ART. "Cæsar, beware of Brutus; take heed of Cassius; come not
   near Casca; have an eye to Cinna; trust not Trebonius;
   mark well Metellus Cimber; Decius Brutus loves thee
   not; thou hast wrong'd Caius Ligarius. There is but one
   mind in all these men, and it is bent against Cæsar. If  5
   thou beest not immortal, look about you. Security gives
   way to conspiracy. The mighty gods defend thee!
         "Thy lover,
          ARTEMIDORUS."

   Here will I stand till Cæsar pass along  10
   And as a suitor will I give him this.
   My heart laments that virtue cannot live
   Out of the teeth of emulation.
   If thou read this, O Cæsar, thou mayst live;
   If not, the Fates with traitors do contrive.  *Exit.* 15

---

been pardoned by Cæsar and restored to civil rights [K]. 114 *strucken* stricken.
119 *to blame* blameworthy. 128 *That every . . . same* that every seeming friend
is not a true friend. 129 *erns* grieves, sorrows.
 II.III. 5 *bent* directed. 6–7 *Security . . . conspiracy* carelessness, or freedom
from anxiety, open a path to the attacks of conspiracy [K]. 8 *lover* devoted friend.
13 *emulation* envious rivalry.

◇◇◇◇◇◇◇◇◇◇◇◇◇◇◇

[SCENE IV. *Before the house of* Brutus.]

*Enter* Portia *and* Lucius.

POR.    I prithee, boy, run to the Senate House.
        Stay not to answer me, but get thee gone!
        Why dost thou stay?

LUC.                            To know my errand, madam.

POR.    I would have had thee there and here again
        Ere I can tell thee what thou shouldst do there.        5
        [*Aside*] O constancy, be strong upon my side,
        Set a huge mountain 'tween my heart and tongue!
        I have a man's mind, but a woman's might.
        How hard it is for women to keep counsel!
        Art thou here yet?

LUC.                            Madam, what should I do?        10
        Run to the Capitol and nothing else?
        And so return to you and nothing else?

POR.    Yes, bring me word, boy, if thy lord look well,
        For he went sickly forth; and take good note
        What Cæsar doth, what suitors press to him.        15
        Hark, boy! What noise is that?

LUC.    I hear none, madam.

POR.                            Prithee listen well.
        I heard a bustling rumour like a fray,
        And the wind brings it from the Capitol.

LUC.    Sooth, madam, I hear nothing.        20

        *Enter the* Soothsayer.

II.iv. 6 *constancy* firmness, self-possession.   8 *might* physical strength.   9 *counsel*
a secret.   18 *bustling rumour* confused noise, hubbub.   37 *more void* more

POR.    Come hither, fellow. Which way hast thou been?

SOOTH.  At mine own house, good lady.

POR.    What is't o'clock?

SOOTH.                    About the ninth hour, lady.

POR.    Is Cæsar yet gone to the Capitol?

SOOTH.  Madam, not yet. I go to take my stand,                25
        To see him pass on to the Capitol.

POR.    Thou hast some suit to Cæsar, hast thou not?

SOOTH.  That I have, lady, if it will please Cæsar
        To be so good to Cæsar as to hear me:
        I shall beseech him to befriend himself.              30

POR.    Why, know'st thou any harm's intended towards him?

SOOTH.  None that I know will be, much that I fear may chance.
        Good morrow to you. Here the street is narrow.
        The throng that follows Cæsar at the heels,
        Of senators, of prætors, common suitors,              35
        Will crowd a feeble man almost to death.
        I'll get me to a place more void and there
        Speak to great Cæsar as he comes along.      *Exit.*

POR.    I must go in. Ay me, how weak a thing
        The heart of woman is! O Brutus,                      40
        The heavens speed thee in thine enterprise!
        Sure the boy heard me. — Brutus hath a suit
        That Cæsar will not grant. — O, I grow faint. —
        Run, Lucius, and commend me to my lord;
        Say I am merry. Come to me again                      45
        And bring me word what he doth say to thee.

                              *Exeunt* [*severally*].

___

empty, less crowded.    41 *speed* prosper.    42–3 *Brutus . . . grant* Spoken to prevent any suspicion on the part of Lucius [K].    45 *merry* in good spirits.

# Act Three

◈◈◈◈◈◈◈◈◈◈◈◈◈◈◈◈◈◈◈◈◈◈◈◈◈◈◈◈◈◈◈◈◈◈◈◈◈◈

[SCENE I. *Rome. A street before the Capitol.*]

*Flourish. Enter* Cæsar, Brutus, Cassius, Casca, Decius,
  Metellus, Trebonius, Cinna, Antony, Lepidus, Artemidorus, [Popilius,] Publius, *and the* Soothsayer.

| | |
|---|---|
| CÆS. | The ides of March are come. |
| SOOTH. | Ay, Cæsar, but not gone. |
| ART. | Hail, Cæsar! Read this schedule. |
| DEC. | Trebonius doth desire you to o'erread |
| | (At your best leisure) this his humble suit. |
| ART. | O Cæsar, read mine first; for mine's a suit |
| | That touches Cæsar nearer. Read it, great Cæsar! |
| CÆS. | What touches us ourself shall be last serv'd. |
| ART. | Delay not, Cæsar! Read it instantly! |
| CÆS. | What, is the fellow mad? |
| PUB. | Sirrah, give place. |
| CASS. | What, urge you your petitions in the street? |
| | Come to the Capitol. |

5

10

[Cæsar *enters the Capitol, the rest fol-*
  *lowing.*]

---

III.i. 3 *schedule* document.    8 *serv'd* attended to. This refusal by Cæsar to read
the notice is Shakespeare's departure from Plutarch.    18 *makes to* makes up to,
approaches.    19 *sudden* prompt. *prevention* being headed off.    22 *constant*
resolute, firm.    24 *change* change countenance.    28 *presently* at once. *prefer his
suit* present his petition.    29 *address'd* ready.    32 *Cæsar and his Senate* The

44

| | |
|---|---|
| POP. | I wish your enterprise to-day may thrive. |
| CASS. | What enterprise, Popilius? |
| POP. | Fare you well. |

*[Advances to* Cæsar.]

| | | |
|---|---|---|
| BRU. | What said Popilius Lena? | 15 |

CASS. He wish'd to-day our enterprise might thrive.
I fear our purpose is discovered.

BRU. Look how he makes to Cæsar. Mark him.

CASS. Casca, be sudden, for we fear prevention.
Brutus, what shall be done? If this be known,                    20
Cassius or Cæsar never shall turn back,
For I will slay myself.

BRU. Cassius, be constant.
Popilius Lena speaks not of our purposes;
For look, he smiles, and Cæsar doth not change.

CASS. Trebonius knows his time; for look you, Brutus,            25
He draws Mark Antony out of the way.

*[Exeunt* Antony *and* Trebonius.]

DEC. Where is Metellus Cimber? Let him go
And presently prefer his suit to Cæsar.

BRU. He is address'd. Press near and second him.

CIN. Casca, you are the first that rears your hand.              30

CÆS. Are we all ready? What is now amiss
That Cæsar and his Senate must redress?

MET. Most high, most mighty, and most puissant Cæsar,
Metellus Cimber throws before thy seat
An humble heart.                                    *[Kneels.]*

CÆS. I must prevent thee, Cimber.                                35
These couchings and these lowly courtesies

---

royal airs which Cæsar gives himself in this scene, though not in accordance with
his historical character, have dramatic propriety. Their purpose is to justify the
act of the conspirators, which, if our sympathies are not on their side, will appear
to be a cowardly assassination [K].    35 *prevent* forestall.    36 *couchings* prostra-
tions, obeisances.

Might fire the blood of ordinary men
And turn preordinance and first decree
Into the law of children. Be not fond
To think that Cæsar bears such rebel blood            40
That will be thaw'd from the true quality
With that which melteth fools — I mean, sweet words,
Low-crooked curtsies, and base spaniel fawning.
Thy brother by decree is banished.
If thou dost bend and pray and fawn for him,          45
I spurn thee like a cur out of my way.
Know, Cæsar doth not wrong, nor without cause
Will he be satisfied.

MET.    Is there no voice more worthy than my own,
To sound more sweetly in great Cæsar's ear            50
For the repealing of my banish'd brother?

BRU.    I kiss thy hand, but not in flattery, Cæsar,
Desiring thee that Publius Cimber may
Have an immediate freedom of repeal.

CÆS.    What, Brutus?

CASS.                Pardon, Cæsar! Cæsar, pardon!     55
As low as to thy foot doth Cassius fall
To beg enfranchisement for Publius Cimber.

CÆS.    I could be well mov'd, if I were as you;
If I could pray to move, prayers would move me:
But I am constant as the Northern Star,               60
Of whose true-fix'd and resting quality
There is no fellow in the firmament.
The skies are painted with unnumb'red sparks,
They are all fire, and every one doth shine;
But there's but one in all doth hold his place.       65

---

38 *preordinance and first decree* settled purpose and decision already made [K].
39 *law of children* fickle law such as may be changed by every whim (*law* JOHN-
SON; F¹: "lane"). *fond* foolish.    40 *rebel blood* a disposition which, on every im-
pulse, rebels against the reason, a fickle or inconstant disposition [K].    41–2
*thaw'd . . . fools* moved from the firmness and stability it should have by such
flattery as can ordinarily influence fools (or children).    43 *spaniel* a dog usually
associated with fawning and flattery.    51 *repealing* recall.    54 *freedom of repeal*
permission to return from banishment.    61 *resting quality* immovable nature.

So in the world: 'Tis furnish'd well with men,
And men are flesh and blood, and apprehensive;
Yet in the number I do know but one
That unassailable holds on his rank,
Unshak'd of motion; and that I am he,                    70
Let me a little show it, even in this —
That I was constant Cimber should be banish'd
And constant do remain to keep him so.

CIN.      O Cæsar!

CÆS.                Hence! Wilt thou lift up Olympus?

DEC.      Great Cæsar!

CÆS.                Doth not Brutus bootless kneel?         75

CASCA.    Speak hands for me!

                *They stab* Cæsar [— Casca *first,* Brutus
                *last*].

CÆS.      Et tu, Brute? — Then fall Cæsar!            *Dies.*

CIN.      Liberty! Freedom! Tyranny is dead!
          Run hence, proclaim, cry it about the streets!

CASS.     Some to the common pulpits and cry out         80
          "Liberty, freedom, and enfranchisement!"

BRU.      People and Senators, be not affrighted.
          Fly not; stand still. Ambition's debt is paid.

CASCA.    Go to the pulpit, Brutus.

DEC.                    And Cassius too.

BRU.      Where's Publius?                                85

CIN.      Here, quite confounded with this mutiny.

---

65 *his* its.   67 *apprehensive* quick to take suggestions; hence, subject to impressions, ruled by their feelings and not by reason [K].   69 *holds on his rank* maintains his stately course [K].   70 *Unshak'd of motion* unshaken either by his own impulses or by external influence [K].   72 *constant* firm, resolute.   74 *lift up Olympus* attempt what is impossible. Mt. Olympus was the home of the Greek gods.   75 *bootless* in vain.   80 *pulpits* rostrums, platforms for public oratory. 83 *Ambition's debt* what was due to ambition. Cæsar's ambition has received its deserts; no other lives are sought [K].   86 *mutiny* uproar, rebellion.

MET.    Stand fast together, lest some friend of Cæsar's
        Should chance —

BRU.    Talk not of standing! Publius, good cheer.
        There is no harm intended to your person                    90
        Nor to no Roman else. So tell them, Publius.

CASS.   And leave us, Publius, lest that the people,
        Rushing on us, should do your age some mischief.

BRU.    Do so; and let no man abide this deed
        But we the doers.

                    *Enter* Trebonius.

CASS.                   Where is Antony?                            95

TREB.   Fled to his house amaz'd.
        Men, wives, and children stare, cry out, and run,
        As it were doomsday.

BRU.                        Fates, we will know your pleasures
        That we shall die, we know; 'tis but the time,
        And drawing days out, that men stand upon.                 100

CASCA.  Why, he that cuts off twenty years of life
        Cuts off so many years of fearing death.

BRU.    Grant that, and then is death a benefit.
        So are we Cæsar's friends, that have abridg'd
        His time of fearing death. Stoop, Romans, stoop,          105
        And let us bathe our hands in Cæsar's blood
        Up to the elbows and besmear our swords.
        Then walk we forth, even to the market place,
        And waving our red weapons o'er our heads,
        Let's all cry "Peace, freedom, and liberty!"              110

CASS.   Stoop then and wash. How many ages hence

---

93 *your age* your aged self.   94 *abide* stand the consequences of.   96 *amaz'd* Not
merely "surprised" or "astonished" in the modern sense but "utterly confounded,
stupefied" [K].   97 *wives* women.   100 *drawing days out* prolonging life. *stand
upon* emphasize.   101 *Casca* F¹; POPE, K assign the speech to Cassius.   108 *market
place* the Forum, which was the centre of Roman business and public life [K].
112 *Shall this . . . acted over* The Elizabethan dramatists are fond of figures
drawn from the stage. Here Cassius seems to predict the writing of the play of
JULIUS CAESAR. Modern critics object to the passage on the ground that it calls

Shall this our lofty scene be acted over
In states unborn and accents yet unknown!

BRU.     How many times shall Cæsar bleed in sport,
That now on Pompey's basis lies along                    115
No worthier than the dust!

CASS.                              So oft as that shall be,
So often shall the knot of us be call'd
The men that gave their country liberty.

DEC.     What, shall we forth?

CASS.                              Ay, every man away.
Brutus shall lead, and we will grace his heels            120
With the most boldest and best hearts of Rome.

*Enter a* Servant.

BRU.     Soft! who comes here? A friend of Antony's.

SERV.    Thus, Brutus, did my master bid me kneel;
Thus did Mark Antony bid me fall down;
And being prostrate, thus he bade me say:                 125
Brutus is noble, wise, valiant, and honest;
Cæsar was mighty, bold, royal, and loving.
Say I love Brutus and I honour him;
Say I fear'd Cæsar, honour'd him, and lov'd him.
If Brutus will vouchsafe that Antony                      130
May safely come to him and be resolv'd
How Cæsar hath deserv'd to lie in death,
Mark Antony shall not love Cæsar dead
So well as Brutus living; but will follow
The fortunes and affairs of noble Brutus                  135
Thorough the hazards of this untrod state

---

attention to the unreality of the spectacle which the audience is beholding. To
the Elizabethans, no doubt, the contrary seemed to be true: by speaking of plays
and acting, the "dramatis personae" appeared to emphasize the idea that they
themselves were real and not mere players [K].    113 *states* F²; F¹ "state."    114 *in
sport* in plays.    115 *basis* pedestal. *lies* F¹; F¹: "lye." *along* at full length,
prostrate.    117 *knot* group.    120 *grace* do honour to.    126 *honest* honourable.
131 *be resolv'd* have his doubts cleared up; receive an explanation [K].    136
*untrod state* novel or untried condition of the commonwealth [K].

With all true faith. So says my master Antony.

BRU.    Thy master is a wise and valiant Roman.
I never thought him worse.
Tell him, so please him come unto this place,     140
He shall be satisfied and, by my honour,
Depart untouch'd.

SERV.          I'll fetch him presently.     *Exit.*

BRU.    I know that we shall have him well to friend.

CASS.    I wish we may. But yet have I a mind
That fears him much; and my misgiving still     145
Falls shrewdly to the purpose.

*Enter* Antony.

BRU.    But here comes Antony. Welcome, Mark Antony.

ANT.    O mighty Cæsar! dost thou lie so low?
Are all thy conquests, glories, triumphs, spoils,
Shrunk to this little measure? Fare thee well.     150
I know not, gentlemen, what you intend,
Who else must be let blood, who else is rank.
If I myself, there is no hour so fit
As Cæsar's death's hour; nor no instrument
Of half that worth as those your swords, made rich     155
With the most noble blood of all this world.
I do beseech ye, if you bear me hard,
Now, whilst your purpled hands do reek and smoke,
Fulfill your pleasure. Live a thousand years,
I shall not find myself so apt to die;     160
No place will please me so, no mean of death,
As here by Cæsar, and by you cut off,
The choice and master spirits of this age.

---

140 *so please him come* if it please him to come.   142 *presently* immediately.
143 *to friend* as a friend.   145–6 *my misgiving . . . purpose* when I have misgiv-
ings, they always prove to be unpleasantly near the truth. Cassius is still uncon-
vinced as to Antony's harmlessness [K].   146 *Falls . . . purpose* hits the mark
exactly.   152 *let blood* killed. *rank* too luxuriant, overgrown in power [K].   157
*bear me hard* have a grudge against me.   158 *purpled* dyed crimson with blood.
160 *apt* ready.   161 *mean of death* manner of dying.   174–5 *Our arms . . . receive you in* our arms, violent in enmity as they seem, and our hearts, which

BRU.    O Antony, beg not your death of us!
    Though now we must appear bloody and cruel,    165
    As by our hands and this our present act
    You see we do, yet see you but our hands
    And this the bleeding business they have done.
    Our hearts you see not. They are pitiful;
    And pity to the general wrong of Rome    170
    (As fire drives out fire, so pity pity)
    Hath done this deed on Cæsar. For your part,
    To you our swords have leaden points, Mark Antony.
    Our arms in strength of malice, and our hearts
    Of brothers' temper, do receive you in    175
    With all kind love, good thoughts, and reverence.

CASS.    Your voice shall be as strong as any man's
    In the disposing of new dignities.

BRU.    Only be patient till we have appeas'd
    The multitude, beside themselves with fear,    180
    And then we will deliver you the cause
    Why I, that did love Cæsar when I struck him,
    Have thus proceeded.

ANT.                    I doubt not of your wisdom.
    Let each man render me his bloody hand.
    First, Marcus Brutus, will I shake with you;    185
    Next, Caius Cassius, do I take your hand;
    Now, Decius Brutus, yours; now yours, Metellus;
    Yours, Cinna; and, my valiant Casca, yours.
    Though last, not least in love, yours, good Trebonius.
    Gentlemen all — Alas, what shall I say?    190
    My credit now stands on such slippery ground
    That one of two bad ways you must conceit me,

---

cherish brotherly feelings toward you, receive you in. "Malice" means simply "enmity." There is the same antithesis between the murderous violence of their "arms" and the brotherly kindness of their "hearts" as in ll. 165–72. Their bloodstained "hands and arms" show their hatred of tyrants, but their "hearts," which have prompted the deed, were actuated by compassion for the wrongs of Rome [K].
177 *Your voice* Cassius has a better knowledge of what motives would appeal to Mark Antony than Brutus has [K].    181 *deliver* report.    191 *credit* reputation.
192 *conceit* conceive of, regard.

Either a coward or a flatterer.
That I did love thee, Cæsar, O, 'tis true!
If then thy spirit look upon us now,                                     195
Shall it not grieve thee dearer than thy death
To see thy Antony making his peace,
Shaking the bloody fingers of thy foes,
Most noble! in the presence of thy corse?
Had I as many eyes as thou hast wounds,                                  200
Weeping as fast as they stream forth thy blood,
It would become me better than to close
In terms of friendship with thine enemies.
Pardon me, Julius! Here wast thou bay'd, brave hart;
Here didst thou fall; and here thy hunters stand,                        205
Sign'd in thy spoil, and crimson'd in thy lethe.
O world, thou wast the forest to this hart;
And this indeed, O world, the heart of thee!
How like a deer, stroken by many princes,
Dost thou here lie!                                                      210

CASS.    Mark Antony —

ANT.                            Pardon me, Caius Cassius.
The enemies of Cæsar shall say this;
Then, in a friend, it is cold modesty.

CASS.    I blame you not for praising Cæsar so;
But what compact mean you to have with us?                               215
Will you be prick'd in number of our friends,
Or shall we on, and not depend on you?

ANT.    Therefore I took your hands; but was indeed
Sway'd from the point by looking down on Cæsar.
Friends am I with you all, and love you all,                             220
Upon this hope, that you shall give me reasons
Why and wherein Cæsar was dangerous.

---

196 *dearer* more keenly.    202 *close* come to terms.    204 *bay'd* trapped like a
hunted animal.    206 *Sign'd in thy spoil* marked with the signs of thy destruction
[K].    *lethe* death, from the river of forgetfulness in the Greek Hades.    207–8
*hart . . . heart of thee* This pun no Elizabethan author could withstand [K].
209 *stroken* struck down (F¹).    212 *shall say* will inevitably say.    213 *cold modesty* calm, dispassionate speech.    216 *prick'd* marked, numbered, counted. It was
customary to check off names or items in a list by making a little puncture in the

BRU.    Or else were this a savage spectacle.
        Our reasons are so full of good regard
        That were you, Antony, the son of Cæsar,                    225
        You should be satisfied.

ANT.                            That's all I seek;
        And am moreover suitor that I may
        Produce his body to the market place
        And in the pulpit, as becomes a friend,
        Speak in the order of his funeral.                          230

BRU.    You shall, Mark Antony.

CASS.                            Brutus, a word with you.
        [*Aside to* Brutus] You know not what you do. Do not
            consent
        That Antony speak in his funeral.
        Know you how much the people may be mov'd
        By that which he will utter?

BRU.    [*Aside to* Cassius]          By your pardon —            235
        I will myself into the pulpit first
        And show the reason of our Cæsar's death.
        What Antony shall speak, I will protest
        He speaks by leave and by permission;
        And that we are contented Cæsar shall                       240
        Have all true rites and lawful ceremonies.
        It shall advantage more than do us wrong.

CASS.   [*Aside to* Brutus] I know not what may fall. I like it not.

BRU.    Mark Antony, here, take you Cæsar's body.
        You shall not in your funeral speech blame us,              245
        But speak all good you can devise of Cæsar;
        And say you do't by our permission.
        Else shall you not have any hand at all

---

paper or parchment with a pin or stylus, or by making a dot with a pen or pencil
[K].    221 *Upon* because of.    224 *so full of good regard* so well-provided with
weighty considerations, so well-considered and convincing [K].    228 *Produce* bring
forward.    230 *order* course.    236 *I will myself* Brutus shows that lofty self-
sufficiency often seen in men of heroic temper, and sometimes amounting to
infatuation [K].    238 *protest* declare.    241 *true* due and proper.    242 *advantage*
benefit.    243 *fall* befall, happen.

|       | About his funeral. And you shall speak |     |
|-------|----------------------------------------|-----|
|       | In the same pulpit whereto I am going, | 250 |
|       | After my speech is ended. |     |
| ANT.  |                Be it so. |     |
|       | I do desire no more. |     |
| BRU.  | Prepare the body then, and follow us. |     |

*Exeunt. Manet* Antony.

| ANT. | O, pardon me, thou bleeding piece of earth, |     |
|------|---------------------------------------------|-----|
|      | That I am meek and gentle with these butchers! | 255 |
|      | Thou art the ruins of the noblest man |     |
|      | That ever lived in the tide of times. |     |
|      | Woe to the hand that shed this costly blood! |     |
|      | Over thy wounds now do I prophesy |     |
|      | (Which, like dumb mouths, do ope their ruby lips | 260 |
|      | To beg the voice and utterance of my tongue), |     |
|      | A curse shall light upon the limbs of men; |     |
|      | Domestic fury and fierce civil strife |     |
|      | Shall cumber all the parts of Italy; |     |
|      | Blood and destruction shall be so in use | 265 |
|      | And dreadful objects so familiar |     |
|      | That mothers shall but smile when they behold |     |
|      | Their infants quartered with the hands of war, |     |
|      | All pity chok'd with custom of fell deeds; |     |
|      | And Cæsar's spirit, ranging for revenge, | 270 |
|      | With Ate by his side come hot from hell, |     |
|      | Shall in these confines with a monarch's voice |     |
|      | Cry "Havoc!" and let slip the dogs of war, |     |

---

257 *tide of times* course of the ages, all history.    260 *dumb mouths* The comparison of wounds to open mouths is common [K].    262 *A curse . . . men* men shall feel in every limb the curse that shall descend to punish what the hands of the conspirators have done. The use of "limbs" is suggested by that of "hand" in l. 258. Not only shall the hands of the murderers be smitten with the curse, but all men's limbs shall share in the punishment [K].    264 *cumber* burden, oppress. 266 *objects* sights.    268 *quartered* cut to pieces.    270 *ranging* roaming up and down like a wild beast in search of prey. Here Antony distinctly prophesies the survival of Cæsar's influence after death and its effect in exacting vengeance from the murderers [K].    271 *Ate* the Greek goddess of discord and vengeance.    273

That this foul deed shall smell above the earth
With carrion men, groaning for burial.                    275

*Enter* Octavius' Servant.

You serve Octavius Cæsar, do you not?

SERV.   I do, Mark Antony.

ANT.    Cæsar did write for him to come to Rome.

SERV.   He did receive his letters and is coming,
And bid me say to you by word of mouth —                  280
O Cæsar!

ANT.    Thy heart is big. Get thee apart and weep.
Passion, I see, is catching; for mine eyes,
Seeing those beads of sorrow stand in thine,
Began to water. Is thy master coming?                     285

SERV.   He lies to-night within seven leagues of Rome.

ANT.    Post back with speed and tell him what hath chanc'd.
Here is a mourning Rome, a dangerous Rome,
No Rome of safety for Octavius yet.
Hie hence and tell him so. Yet stay awhile.               290
Thou shalt not back till I have borne this corse
Into the market place. There shall I try
In my oration how the people take
The cruel issue of these bloody men;
According to the which thou shalt discourse               295
To young Octavius of the state of things.
Lend me your hand.

*Exeunt* [*with* Cæsar's *body*].

---

*Havoc* the cry equivalent to "No quarter!" It was used to proclaim general slaughter and pillage [K].    282 *big* swelling with grief.    283 *Passion* sorrow.    286 *lies* lodges, is encamped. As a matter of fact, Octavius was in Illyria and did not reach Rome for about six weeks. Shakespeare, for dramatic purposes, hastens his arrival and invents the incident of a letter from Julius Cæsar (line 278) to account for his being so near the city [K].    289 *No Rome of safety* An obvious pun, "Rome" being pronounced like "room" [K].    294 *cruel . . . men* the cruel deed resulting from their savage nature. "Issue" is common in the sense of "progeny" and also of "result" [K].

◇◇◇◇◇◇◇◇◇◇◇◇◇◇◇◇

[SCENE II. *Rome. The Forum.*]

*Enter* Brutus *and* Cassius, *with the* Plebeians.

PLEBS.     We will be satisfied! Let us be satisfied!

BRU.     Then follow me and give me audience, friends.
Cassius, go you into the other street
And part the numbers.
Those that will hear me speak, let 'em stay here;          5
Those that will follow Cassius, go with him;
And public reasons shall be rendered
Of Cæsar's death.

1. PLEB.                    I will hear Brutus speak.

2. PLEB.  I will hear Cassius, and compare their reasons
When severally we hear them rendered.                    10

               [*Exit* Cassius, *with some of the* Ple-
               bians.] Brutus *goes into the pulpit.*

3. PLEB.  The noble Brutus is ascended. Silence!

BRU.     Be patient till the last.
Romans, countrymen, and lovers, hear me for my cause,
and be silent, that you may hear. Believe me for mine
honour, and have respect to mine honour, that you may    15
believe. Censure me in your wisdom, and awake your
senses, that you may the better judge. If there be any in
this assembly, any dear friend of Cæsar's, to him I say
that Brutus' love to Cæsar was no less than his. If then
that friend demand why Brutus rose against Cæsar, this    20
is my answer: Not that I lov'd Cæsar less, but that I lov'd
Rome more. Had you rather Cæsar were living, and die
all slaves, than that Cæsar were dead, to live all freemen?

---

III.II. 1 *satisfied* fully informed.    10 *severally* separately.    12 *the last* the con-
clusion of my speech.    13 *Romans, countrymen* It has been remarked that in this
speech Shakespeare aims to reproduce the actual style of Brutus, which, as we
learn on ancient authority, was dry, abrupt, and unadorned. The fact that his
oration is in prose brings out these qualities farther, and emphasizes the contrast
between the diction of Brutus and the warm, fluent and flexible style of Mark
Antony [K].    15 *respect . . . honour* regard to the fact that I am honourable.
16 *Censure* judge.    17 *senses* intellectual powers. Brutus deliberately addresses

As Cæsar lov'd me, I weep for him; as he was fortunate,
I rejoice at it; as he was valiant, I honour him; but — as    25
he was ambitious, I slew him. There is tears for his love;
joy for his fortune; honour for his valour; and death
for his ambition. Who is here so base that would be a
bondman? If any, speak; for him have I offended. Who
is here so rude that would not be a Roman? If any,    30
speak; for him have I offended. Who is here so vile that
will not love his country? If any, speak; for him have I
offended. I pause for a reply.

ALL.    None, Brutus, none!

BRU.    Then none have I offended. I have done no more to    35
Cæsar than you shall do to Brutus. The question of his
death is enroll'd in the Capitol; his glory not extenuated,
wherein he was worthy; nor his offences enforc'd, for
which he suffered death.

> *Enter* Mark Antony [*and others*], *with*
> Cæsar's *body.*

Here comes his body, mourn'd by Mark Antony, who,    40
though he had no hand in his death, shall receive the
benefit of his dying, a place in the commonwealth, as
which of you shall not? With this I depart, that, as I
slew my best lover for the good of Rome, I have the same
dagger for myself when it shall please my country to need    45
my death.

ALL.    Live, Brutus! live, live!

1. PLEB.    Bring him with triumph home unto his house.

2. PLEB.    Give him a statue with his ancestors.

3. PLEB.    Let him be Cæsar.

4. PLEB.    Cæsar's better parts    50

---

the minds of his hearers, not their passions [K].    30 *rude* boorish and ignorant
[K].    36–7 *The question . . . enroll'd* the whole matter of his death is on record
[K].    38 *enforc'd* dwelled upon.    42 *place in the commonwealth* free citizenship;
a citizen's place in the free state. The implication is that in Cæsar's lifetime all
Romans were subjects or slaves [K].    44 *best lover* closest friend.    49 *Give . . .
ancestors* in particular, with Lucius Junius Brutus, the Liberator [K].    50 *Let him
be Cæsar* There is unconscious irony in the citizen's cry. He shows how little he
understands free citizenship [K].    *parts* qualities.

Shall be crown'd in Brutus.

1. PLEB. We'll bring him to his house with shouts and clamours.

BRU.    My countrymen —

2. PLEB.                    Peace! silence! Brutus speaks.

1. PLEB. Peace, ho!

BRU.    Good countrymen, let me depart alone,                    55
        And, for my sake, stay here with Antony.
        Do grace to Cæsar's corpse, and grace his speech
        Tending to Cæsar's glories which Mark Antony,
        By our permission, is allow'd to make.
        I do entreat you, not a man depart,                      60
        Save I alone, till Antony have spoke.        *Exit.*

1. PLEB. Stay, ho! and let us hear Mark Antony.

3. PLEB. Let him go up into the public chair.
        We'll hear him. Noble Antony, go up.

ANT.    For Brutus' sake I am beholding to you.      [*Goes up.*] 65

4. PLEB. What does he say of Brutus?

3. PLEB.                            He says for Brutus' sake
        He finds himself beholding to us all.

4. PLEB. 'Twere best he speak no harm of Brutus here!

1. PLEB. This Cæsar was a tyrant.

3. PLEB.                        Nay, that's certain.
        We are blest that Rome is rid of him.                    70

2. PLEB. Peace! Let us hear what Antony can say.

ANT.    You gentle Romans —

ALL.                        Peace, ho! Let us hear him.

ANT.    Friends, Romans, countrymen, lend me your ears;
        I come to bury Cæsar, not to praise him.
        The evil that men do lives after them;                   75

57 *Do . . . speech* do respect to Cæsar's body, and honour Antony's address (by
your presence) [K].    63 *public chair* pulpit, rostrum.    65 *beholding* beholden,
obliged.    69 *a tyrant* a usurping tyrant. The word commonly carried with it the

The good is oft interred with their bones.
So let it be with Cæsar. The noble Brutus
Hath told you Cæsar was ambitious.
If it were so, it was a grievous fault,
And grievously hath Cæsar answer'd it.                80
Here, under leave of Brutus and the rest
(For Brutus is an honourable man;
So are they all, all honourable men),
Come I to speak in Cæsar's funeral.
He was my friend, faithful and just to me;            85
But Brutus says he was ambitious,
And Brutus is an honourable man.
He hath brought many captives home to Rome,
Whose ransoms did the general coffers fill.
Did this in Cæsar seem ambitious?                     90
When that the poor have cried, Cæsar hath wept;
Ambition should be made of sterner stuff.
Yet Brutus says he was ambitious;
And Brutus is an honourable man.
You all did see that on the Lupercal                  95
I thrice presented him a kingly crown,
Which he did thrice refuse. Was this ambition?
Yet Brutus says he was ambitious;
And sure he is an honourable man.
I speak not to disprove what Brutus spoke,            100
But here I am to speak what I do know.
You all did love him once, not without cause.
What cause withholds you then to mourn for him?
O judgment, thou art fled to brutish beasts,
And men have lost their reason! Bear with me.         105
My heart is in the coffin there with Cæsar,
And I must pause till it come back to me.

1. PLEB. Methinks there is much reason in his sayings.

2. PLEB. If thou consider rightly of the matter,

---

idea of royal power unlawfully obtained [K].   72 *gentle Romans* gentlemen of
Rome.   80 *answer'd* paid for.   85 *just* exact and punctual in all the duties of
friendship [K].   89 *general coffers* public treasury.   104 *art* F²; F¹: "are."

Cæsar has had great wrong.

3. PLEB.                    Has he not, masters?    110
I fear there will a worse come in his place.

4. PLEB. Mark'd ye his words? He would not take the crown;
Therefore 'tis certain he was not ambitious.

1. PLEB. If it be found so, some will dear abide it.

2. PLEB. Poor soul! his eyes are red as fire with weeping.    115

3. PLEB. There's not a nobler man in Rome than Antony.

4. PLEB. Now mark him. He begins again to speak.

ANT.    But yesterday the word of Cæsar might
Have stood against the world. Now lies he there,
And none so poor to do him reverence.    120
O masters! If I were dispos'd to stir
Your hearts and minds to mutiny and rage,
I should do Brutus wrong, and Cassius wrong,
Who, you all know, are honourable men.
I will not do them wrong. I rather choose    125
To wrong the dead, to wrong myself and you,
Than I will wrong such honourable men.
But here's a parchment with the seal of Cæsar.
I found it in his closet; 'tis his will.
Let but the commons hear this testament,    130
Which (pardon me) I do not mean to read,
And they would go and kiss dead Cæsar's wounds
And dip their napkins in his sacred blood;
Yea, beg a hair of him for memory,
And dying, mention it within their wills,    135
Bequeathing it as a rich legacy
Unto their issue.

4. PLEB. We'll hear the will! Read it, Mark Antony.

ALL.    The will, the will! We will hear Cæsar's will!

---

110 *not* CRAIK; not in F¹.    114 *dear abide* pay dearly for.    120 *to do* as to do.
122 *mutiny* riot and disorder.    129 *closet* private room.    133 *napkins* handkerchiefs. The line refers to the custom of dipping cloths in the blood of martyrs
and preserving them as precious and even medicinal relics [K].    145 *'Tis good*

ANT.    Have patience, gentle friends; I must not read it.                    140
It is not meet you know how Cæsar lov'd you.
You are not wood, you are not stones, but men;
And being men, hearing the will of Cæsar,
It will inflame you, it will make you mad.
'Tis good you know not that you are his heirs;                    145
For if you should, O, what would come of it?

4. PLEB.    Read the will! We'll hear it, Antony!
You shall read us the will, Cæsar's will!

ANT.    Will you be patient? Will you stay awhile?
I have o'ershot myself to tell you of it.                    150
I fear I wrong the honourable men
Whose daggers have stabb'd Cæsar; I do fear it.

4. PLEB.    They were traitors. Honourable men!

ALL.    The will! the testament!

2. PLEB.    They were villains, murderers! The will! Read the will!    155

ANT.    You will compel me then to read the will?
Then make a ring about the corpse of Cæsar
And let me show you him that made the will.
Shall I descend? and will you give me leave?

ALL.    Come down.                    160

2. PLEB.    Descend.

3. PLEB.    You shall have leave.            [Antony *comes down.*]

4. PLEB.    A ring! Stand round.

1. PLEB.    Stand from the hearse! Stand from the body!

2. PLEB.    Room for Antony, most noble Antony!                    165

ANT.    Nay, press not so upon me. Stand far off.

ALL.    Stand back! Room! Bear back!

ANT.    If you have tears, prepare to shed them now.

---

. . . *heirs* Antony discloses the main fact about the will by the very words of his
refusal to read it [K].    150 *o'ershot myself* shot beyond the mark; gone farther
than I intended. A figure from archery [K].    164 *hearse* bier.    167 *Bear* move.

You all do know this mantle. I remember
The first time ever Cæsar put it on.                            170
'Twas on a summer's evening in his tent,
That day he overcame the Nervii.
Look, in this place ran Cassius' dagger through.
See what a rent the envious Casca made.
Through this the well-beloved Brutus stabb'd;                   175
And as he pluck'd his cursed steel away,
Mark how the blood of Cæsar followed it,
As rushing out of doors to be resolv'd
If Brutus so unkindly knock'd or no;
For Brutus, as you know, was Cæsar's angel.                     180
Judge, O you gods, how dearly Cæsar lov'd him!
This was the most unkindest cut of all;
For when the noble Cæsar saw him stab,
Ingratitude, more strong than traitors' arms,
Quite vanquish'd him. Then burst his mighty heart;             185
And in his mantle muffling up his face,
Even at the base of Pompey's statuë
(Which all the while ran blood) great Cæsar fell.
O, what a fall was there, my countrymen!
Then I, and you, and all of us fell down,                       190
Whilst bloody treason flourish'd over us.
O, now you weep, and I perceive you feel
The dint of pity. These are gracious drops.
Kind souls, what weep you when you but behold
Our Cæsar's vesture wounded? Look you here!                     195
Here is himself, marr'd as you see with traitors.

1. PLEB.  O piteous spectacle!

---

169 *this mantle* Shakespeare disregards niceties of Roman costume. The toga that
Cæsar wore at the time of his assassination was something quite different from
the "paludamentum," or military cloak [K].    172 *Nervii* Cæsar overcame the Nervii,
a warlike tribe of Belgic Gaul in 57 B.C., thirteen years before his death. His
victory had been celebrated at Rome by an unprecedented thanksgiving. Antony
was not with him in this campaign. He visited Cæsar in Gaul in 54 B.C. Shakespeare uses poetic license, as always in dramatizing historical details [K].    174
*envious* malicious.    178 *be resolv'd* have all doubts cleared up.    180 *angel* dearest
friend. It was in reality Decimus Brutus (Shakespeare's Decius) — not Marcus —
who was a particular friend of Cæsar's [K].    191 *flourish'd* triumphed.    193 *dint*
stroke.  *gracious* either (a) honourable or (b) becoming. The sense is practically

2. PLEB.  O noble Cæsar!

3. PLEB.  O woful day!

4. PLEB.  O traitors, villains!                                    200

1. PLEB.  O most bloody sight!

2. PLEB.  We will be reveng'd.

ALL.     Revenge! About! Seek! Burn! Fire!
         Kill! Slay! Let not a traitor live!

ANT.     Stay, countrymen.                                         205

1. PLEB.  Peace there! Hear the noble Antony.

2. PLEB.  We'll hear him, we'll follow him, we'll die with him!

ANT.     Good friends, sweet friends, let me not stir you up
         To such a sudden flood of mutiny.
         They that have done this deed are honourable.          210
         What private griefs they have, alas, I know not,
         That made them do it. They are wise and honourable,
         And will no doubt with reasons answer you.
         I come not, friends, to steal away your hearts.
         I am no orator, as Brutus is,                          215
         But (as you know me all) a plain blunt man
         That love my friend; and that they know full well
         That gave me public leave to speak of him.
         For I have neither wit, nor words, nor worth,
         Action, nor utterance, nor the power of speech          220
         To stir men's blood. I only speak right on.
         I tell you that which you yourselves do know,
         Show you sweet Cæsar's wounds, poor poor dumb mouths,

---

the same in either case: "tears that do credit to your good feeling and soundness
of heart" [K].    194 *what* why.    209 *mutiny* disorder, riot.    211 *griefs* grievances.
Antony artfully suggests that there can have been no public reason for the murder
of Cæsar, and that the conspirators were actuated by motives of private vengeance
[K].    216 *blunt* simple and forthright, without mental acuteness.    219 *wit* F²; F¹:
"writ."    219-21 *For I . . . blood* A complete list of the qualities of a good orator:
(1) intellectual cleverness (wit); (2) fluency (words); (3) "auctoritas," the weight that
comes from character or standing (worth); (4) gesture and bearing (action); (5)
skillful elocution, good delivery (utterance) — and finally (6) the power of speech
to stir men's blood, without which all other accomplishments avail but little [K].

And bid them speak for me. But were I Brutus,
And Brutus Antony, there were an Antony                      225
Would ruffle up your spirits, and put a tongue
In every wound of Cæsar that should move
The stones of Rome to rise and mutiny.

ALL.      We'll mutiny.

1. PLEB.   We'll burn the house of Brutus.                   230

3. PLEB.   Away then! Come, seek the conspirators.

ANT.      Yet hear me, countrymen. Yet hear me speak.

ALL.      Peace, ho! Hear Antony, most noble Antony!

ANT.      Why, friends, you go to do you know not what.
Wherein hath Cæsar thus deserv'd your loves?                 235
Alas, you know not! I must tell you then.
You have forgot the will I told you of.

ALL.      Most true! The will! Let's stay and hear the will.

ANT.      Here is the will, and under Cæsar's seal.
To every Roman citizen he gives,                             240
To every several man, seventy-five drachmas.

2. PLEB.   Most noble Cæsar! We'll revenge his death!

3. PLEB.   O royal Cæsar!

ANT.      Hear me with patience.

ALL.      Peace, ho!                                         245

ANT.      Moreover, he hath left you all his walks,
His private arbours, and new-planted orchards,
On this side Tiber; he hath left them you,
And to your heirs for ever — common pleasures,

---

226 *ruffle up* rouse to madness. The word was much stronger than to-day. A
"ruffler" was a quarrelsome ruffian [K].    241 *drachmas* The drachma is usually
rated at about nineteen cents, but the purchasing power of money was so great in
ancient times that this gives little idea of its value [K].    247 *orchards* gardens.
249 *pleasures* pleasure grounds.    258 *forms* long benches.   *windows* shutters.
263 *Lepidus* Marcus Aemilius Lepidus, a partisan of Cæsar, was outside Rome
with an army at the time of the murder. In the course of the next night he en-
tered the city with his troops and thus became a person of importance in the
events that followed [K].    265 *upon a wish* just when he is wanted; most oppor-

To walk abroad and recreate yourselves.                    250
Here was a Cæsar! When comes such another?

1. PLEB. Never, never! Come, away, away!
We'll burn his body in the holy place
And with the brands fire the traitors' houses.
Take up the body.                                          255

2. PLEB. Go fetch fire!

3. PLEB. Pluck down benches!

4. PLEB. Pluck down forms, windows, anything!

*Exeunt* Plebeians [*with the body*].

ANT. Now let it work. Mischief, thou art afoot,
Take thou what course thou wilt.

*Enter* Servant.

How now, fellow?     260

SERV. Sir, Octavius is already come to Rome.

ANT. Where is he?

SERV. He and Lepidus are at Cæsar's house.

ANT. And thither will I straight to visit him.
He comes upon a wish. Fortune is merry,            265
And in this mood will give us anything.

SERV. I heard him say Brutus and Cassius
Are rid like madmen through the gates of Rome.

ANT. Belike they had some notice of the people
How I had mov'd them. Bring me to Octavius.        270

*Exeunt.*

tunely. As a matter of history, Antony was not much pleased at the coming of
Octavius, for he had affairs more or less under his own control [K].     266 *mood*
That Fortune's mood is favourable is shown by the opportune arrival of Octavius.
The personification of Fortune is one of the most striking conventions of ancient
and medieval thought, and it descended in full force to the Elizabethans, partly
from the Middle Ages and partly from direct imitation of the classics [K].     269
*Belike* probably.     269-70 *some notice . . . them* some notice of how I had
moved the people.

◇◇◇◇◇◇◇◇◇◇◇◇◇◇◇◇

[SCENE III. *Rome. A street.*]

*Enter* CINNA *the Poet, and after him the* Plebeians.

CIN.    I dreamt to-night that I did feast with Cæsar,
        And things unluckily charge my fantasy.
        I have no will to wander forth of doors,
        Yet something leads me forth.

1. PLEB.  What is your name?                                  5

2. PLEB.  Whither are you going?

3. PLEB.  Where do you dwell?

4. PLEB.  Are you a married man or a bachelor?

2. PLEB.  Answer every man directly.

1. PLEB.  Ay, and briefly.                                    10

4. PLEB.  Ay, and wisely.

3. PLEB.  Ay, and truly, you were best.

CIN.    What is my name? Whither am I going? Where do I
        dwell? Am I a married man or a bachelor? Then, to
        answer every man directly and briefly, wisely and truly:  15
        wisely I say, I am a bachelor.

2. PLEB.  That's as much as to say they are fools that marry. You'll
        bear me a bang for that, I fear. Proceed — directly.

CIN.    Directly I am going to Cæsar's funeral.

III.iii. This scene takes place on the same day as Scene ii. The incident is reported
by Suetonius and Plutarch as occurring immediately after Cæsar's funeral. C.
Helvius Cinna was a friend of Catullus and a poet of distinction in his day. Only
a few lines of his verse have survived [K].   1 *to-night* last night.   2 *things . . .
fantasy* the events that have happened oppress my imagination with forebodings.
Since "dreams go by contraries," it was thought to be unlucky to dream of feasting,
and to dream of feasting with Cæsar would be especially ominous under the cir-
cumstances [K].   3 *of doors* away from home.   9 *directly* plainly, to the point.
18 *bear me a bang* get a knock from me.

| | |
|---|---|
| 1. PLEB. | As a friend or an enemy? |

20

CIN.     As a friend.

2. PLEB. That matter is answered directly.

4. PLEB. For your dwelling — briefly.

CIN.     Briefly, I dwell by the Capitol.

3. PLEB. Your name, sir, truly.

25

CIN.     Truly, my name is Cinna.

1. PLEB. Tear him to pieces! He's a conspirator.

CIN.     I am Cinna the poet! I am Cinna the poet!

4. PLEB. Tear him for his bad verses! Tear him for his bad verses!

CIN.     I am not Cinna the conspirator.

30

4. PLEB. It is no matter; his name's Cinna! Pluck but his name out of his heart, and turn him going.

3. PLEB. Tear him, tear him! Come, brands, ho! firebrands! To Brutus', to Cassius'! Burn all! Some to Decius' house and some to Casca's; some to Ligarius'! Away, go!

35

*Exeunt all the* Plebeians [*with* Cinna].

# Act Four

◇◇◇◇◇◇◇◇◇◇◇◇◇◇◇◇◇◇◇◇◇◇◇◇◇◇◇◇◇◇◇◇◇◇◇◇◇◇◇◇◇◇◇◇◇◇◇◇◇◇◇

[SCENE I. *Rome*. Antony's *house*.]

*Enter* Antony, Octavius, *and* Lepidus.

ANT.   These many, then, shall die; their names are prick'd.

OCT.   Your brother too must die. Consent you, Lepidus?

LEP.   I do consent —

OCT.                        Prick him down, Antony.

LEP.   Upon condition Publius shall not live,
Who is your sister's son, Mark Antony.                          5

ANT.   He shall not live. Look, with a spot I damn him.
But, Lepidus, go you to Cæsar's house.
Fetch the will hither, and we shall determine
How to cut off some charge in legacies.

LEP.   What? shall I find you here?                          10

OCT.   Or here or at the Capitol.            *Exit* Lepidus.

ANT.   This is a slight unmeritable man,

---

IV.I. 1–2 *These many . . . prick'd* The Triumvirs have all but finished their business of proscription when the scene opens. Antony holds the list of hostile or suspected persons and has been pricking the names on which they agree, i.e. marking them with a puncture or dot. The horror of the whole business comes out vividly in the indifference with which Antony sacrifices his own nephew, and Lepidus his own brother [K].    5 *sister's son* Antony had no nephew Publius. His uncle Lucius Cæsar (his mother's brother) was among those proscribed, as Shakespeare must have known from Plutarch. There is no telling whether the dramatist made a mistake here, or whether his departure from history is intentional. Both the brother of Lepidus and Antony's uncle were finally spared [K].    6 *He shall . . . him* It is not Shakespeare's purpose that we should take sides with the Triumvirs,

Meet to be sent on errands. Is it fit,
The threefold world divided, he should stand
One of the three to share it?

OCT.                          So you thought him,                     15
And took his voice who should be prick'd to die
In our black sentence and proscription.

ANT.   Octavius, I have seen more days than you;
And though we lay these honours on this man
To ease ourselves of divers sland'rous loads,          20
He shall but bear them as the ass bears gold,
To groan and sweat under the business,
Either led or driven as we point the way;
And having brought our treasure where we will,
Then take we down his load, and turn him off         25
(Like to the empty ass) to shake his ears
And graze in commons.

OCT.                          You may do your will;
But he's a tried and valiant soldier.

ANT.   So is my horse, Octavius, and for that
I do appoint him store of provender.                         30
It is a creature that I teach to fight,
To wind, to stop, to run directly on,
His corporal motion govern'd by my spirit.
And, in some taste, is Lepidus but so.
He must be taught, and train'd, and bid go forth:        35
A barren-spirited fellow; one that feeds

---

and he thus, by a mere touch, alienates the sympathy and admiration which we
may have acquired for Antony in the preceding act [K]. *damn* condemn.   9 *cut
. . . legacies* reduce expenditure by killing those to whom money has been left.
12 *slight unmeritable* of slight account, and undeserving [K].   14 *threefold world*
Europe, Africa and Asia.   16 *voice* opinion.   20 *sland'rous loads* burdens of
shame.   26 *empty* without his load.   27 *in commons* Common lands for pas-
turage were, in Shakespeare's day, adjacent to most villages, and the horse or
donkey out of work and grazing on what he could find there was a familiar
figure [K].   30 *appoint* assign.   *store* plenty, supply.   32 *wind* turn (like a horse).
33 *spirit* mind.   34 *taste* extent, degree.   36 *barren-spirited* of unproductive
mind, without ideas of his own [K].

On objects, arts, and imitations
Which, out of use and stal'd by other men
Begin his fashion. Do not talk of him,
But as a property. And now, Octavius,                    40
Listen great things. Brutus and Cassius
Are levying powers. We must straight make head.
Therefore let our alliance be combin'd,
Our best friends made, our means stretch'd;
And let us presently go sit in council                    45
How covert matters may be best disclos'd
And open perils surest answered.

OCT.    Let us do so; for we are at the stake
And bay'd about with many enemies;
And some that smile have in their hearts, I fear,         50
Millions of mischiefs.                        *Exeunt.*

◇◇◇◇◇◇◇◇◇◇◇◇◇◇◇◇

[SCENE II.
*The camp near Sardis. Before the tent of* Brutus.]

*Drum. Enter* Brutus, Lucilius, [Lucius,] *and the* Army.
Titinius *and* Pindarus *meet them.*

BRU.    Stand ho!

LUCIL.    Give the word, ho! and stand!

---

37 *objects . . . imitations* The point is that all the "objects" that busy Lepidus,
all the "arts" of life which he practises, and even all the "imitations" (the mere
"fashions") which he undertakes to copy in his turn, are such as have long ago
lost their freshness and interest for other people. He is a tardy copyist of other
men, not only in their "objects" and "arts" but even in their "imitations" [K].
38 *stal'd* cheapened.    40 *property* a thing or utensil; a mere tool, as opposed to
a "person" [K]. 42 *powers* troops. *make head* gather soldiers.    44 *made* mustered.
*our means stretch'd* our resources used to the utmost (F¹; F², K: "and our best
means stretch'd out"). The F² reading is preferred by some editors as metrically
more perfect, but imperfect lines are common in Shakespeare, and the F¹ reading
has far greater authority.    45 *presently* without delay.    46–7 *How . . . answered* how hidden (covert) matters may best be discovered and how obvious
dangers (open perils) may best be met (answered).    48 *we are at the stake* The

BRU.    What now, Lucilius? Is Cassius near?

LUCIL.   He is at hand, and Pindarus is come
         To do you salutation from his master.                    5

BRU.    He greets me well. Your master, Pindarus,
         In his own change, or by ill officers,
         Hath given me some worthy cause to wish
         Things done undone; but if he be at hand,
         I shall be satisfied.

PIN.                  I do not doubt                              10
         But that my noble master will appear
         Such as he is, full of regard and honour.

BRU.    He is not doubted. A word, Lucilius,
         How he receiv'd you. Let me be resolv'd.

LUCIL.   With courtesy and with respect enough,                  15
         But not with such familiar instances
         Nor with such free and friendly conference
         As he hath us'd of old.

BRU.                     Thou hast describ'd
         A hot friend cooling. Ever note, Lucilius,
         When love begins to sicken and decay                    20
         It useth an enforced ceremony.
         There are no tricks in plain and simple faith;
         But hollow men, like horses hot at hand,
         Make gallant show and promise of their mettle;
                                   *Low march within.*
         But when they should endure the bloody spur,            25

---

figure comes from the favourite Elizabethan sport of bear-baiting. They are like
the bear chained to his stake. The dogs are barking about them, eager for the
attack, but still on the leash [K].

  IV.II. 6 *greets me well* sends me greetings by a good man.    7 *In his own* . . .
*officers* whether from a change in his own feelings towards me or because of the
acts of unworthy subordinates [K].   8 *worthy* justifiable.   9 *undone* not done.
10 *be satisfied* receive an explanation.   11–12 *will appear* . . . *honour* when
you talk with him, you will find that he has acted with due regard both to your
wishes and to his own honour [K].   15 *respect* attention.   16 *familiar instances*
proofs of friendship.   17 *conference* conversation.   21 *enforced*, forced, con-
strained.   22 *tricks* artifices.   23 *hollow* insincere. *hot at hand* full of spirit when
held in; restless or impetuous when curbed [K]. The figure is from horsemanship.
24 *mettle* high spirit.

They fall their crests, and like deceitful jades
Sink in the trial. Comes his army on?

LUCIL.    They mean this night in Sardis to be quarter'd.
The greater part, the horse in general,
Are come with Cassius.

BRU.                          Hark! He is arriv'd.                    30
March gently on to meet him.

*Enter* Cassius *and his* Powers.

CASS.    Stand, ho!

BRU.    Stand, ho! Speak the word along.

1. SOLD.    Stand!

2. SOLD.    Stand!                                                   35

3. SOLD.    Stand!

CASS.    Most noble brother, you have done me wrong.

BRU.    Judge me, you gods! wrong I mine enemies?
And if not so, how should I wrong a brother?

CASS.    Brutus, this sober form of yours hides wrongs;          40
And when you do them —

BRU.                          Cassius, be content.
Speak your griefs softly. I do know you well.
Before the eyes of both our armies here
(Which should perceive nothing but love from us)
Let us not wrangle. Bid them move away.                          45
Then in my tent, Cassius, enlarge your griefs,
And I will give you audience.

CASS.                          Pindarus,
Bid our commanders lead their charges off
A little from this ground.

---

26 *fall* let fall. *crests* necks (of horses). *jades* horses (a contemptuous term).    27
*Sink* give way, fail.    29 *horse* cavalry.    31 *gently* slowly.    40 *sober form* grave
demeanour. The habitual gravity and self-restraint of Brutus's demeanour, just
shown in his reply, irritate Cassius all the more because he feels that they contrast unfavourably with his own impatience [K].    41 *be content* calm yourself.

BRU.    Lucilius, do you the like; and let no man      50
       Come to our tent till we have done our conference.
       Let Lucius and Titinius guard our door.      *Exeunt.*

◇◇◇◇◇◇◇◇◇◇◇◇◇◇◇◇◇

[SCENE III.
*The camp near Sardis. Within the tent of* Bru-
     tus.]

*Enter* Brutus *and* Cassius.

CASS.    That you have wrong'd me doth appear in this:
       You have condemn'd and noted Lucius Pella
       For taking bribes here of the Sardians;
       Wherein my letters, praying on his side,
       Because I knew the man, were slighted off.      5

BRU.    You wrong'd yourself to write in such a case.

CASS.    In such a time as this it is not meet
       That every nice offence should bear his comment.

BRU.    Let me tell you, Cassius, you yourself
       Are much condemn'd to have an itching palm,      10
       To sell and mart your offices for gold
       To undeservers.

CASS.            I an itching palm?
       You know that you are Brutus that speaks this,
       Or, by the gods, this speech were else your last!

BRU.    The name of Cassius honours this corruption,      15
       And chastisement doth therefore hide his head.

CASS.    Chastisement?

BRU.    Remember March; the ides of March remember.
       Did not great Julius bleed for justice sake?

---

42 *griefs* grievances.    46 *enlarge* express freely.    48 *charges* troops.

   IV.III. 2 *noted* marked with infamy, disgraced (the Latin "notare").    5 *slighted off* disregarded, put aside with scant attention.    8 *nice offence* trivial fault. *his comment* its criticism or censure.    10 *condemn'd to have* accused of having. *itching palm* covetous disposition.    11 *mart* traffic in.

What villain touch'd his body that did stab 20
And not for justice? What, shall one of us,
That struck the foremost man of all this world
But for supporting robbers — shall we now
Contaminate our fingers with base bribes,
And sell the mighty space of our large honours 25
For so much trash as may be grasped thus?
I had rather be a dog and bay the moon
Than such a Roman.

CASS.                    Brutus, bait not me!
I'll not endure it. You forget yourself
To hedge me in. I am a soldier, I, 30
Older in practice, abler than yourself
To make conditions.

BRU.                    Go to! You are not, Cassius.

CASS. I am.

BRU. I say you are not.

CASS. Urge me no more! I shall forget myself. 35
Have mind upon your health. Tempt me no farther.

BRU. Away, slight man!

CASS. Is't possible?

BRU.                    Hear me, for I will speak.
Must I give way and room to your rash choler?
Shall I be frighted when a madman stares? 40

CASS. O ye gods, ye gods! Must I endure all this?

23 *But . . . robbers* It has often been noticed that this was not the cause which prompted Brutus to attack Cæsar. Extortion, however, is always an accompaniment of tyranny, so that this particular motive may well be regarded as involved in the general one. Besides, Brutus is getting angry, and anger is seldom minutely accurate [k]. By "robbers" he may mean those who would deprive the Romans of their liberty. 25 *mighty . . . honours* our power to confer honourable public offices. 26 *trash* money. 27 *bay the moon* A proverbial phrase for ridiculous futility [k]. 28 *bait* harass. 30 *hedge me in* limit my authority. 32 *make conditions* settle the terms in any negotiations — hence, in a more general sense, to manage affairs [k]. 36 *health* safety and welfare. 37 *slight man* frivolous man, trifler. A word of outspoken insult, which reduces Cassius to almost speechless amazement. He is so astonished at this outburst from grave and philosophic Brutus that he almost forgets to be angry [k]. 39 *give . . . choler* allow free

BRU.    All this? Ay, more! Fret till your proud heart break.
Go show your slaves how choleric you are
And make your bondmen tremble. Must I budge?
Must I observe you? Must I stand and crouch                 45
Under your testy humour? By the gods,
You shall digest the venom of your spleen,
Though it do split you; for from this day forth
I'll use you for my mirth, yea, for my laughter,
When you are waspish.

CASS.                         Is it come to this?                 50

BRU.    You say you are a better soldier.
Let it appear so; make your vaunting true,
And it shall please me well. For mine own part,
I shall be glad to learn of noble men.

CASS.    You wrong me every way! You wrong me, Brutus!         55
I said an elder soldier, not a better.
Did I say "better"?

BRU.                         If you did, I care not.

CASS.    When Cæsar liv'd he durst not thus have mov'd me.

BRU.    Peace, peace! You durst not so have tempted him.

CASS.    I durst not?                                           60

BRU.    No.

CASS.    What, durst not tempt him?

BRU.                         For your life you durst not.

course and scope to your quick temper [K].    43 *choleric* prone to anger.    45 *observe you* show you reverence; be obsequious to you.    47 *digest . . . spleen* The spleen was supposed to be the seat of various sudden fits of emotion, such as uncontrollable laughter, irascibility, nervousness and the like. The exact meaning of the passage is: "When the action of your spleen produces irritation in your mind, you shall not relieve yourself by expressing it, but you shall keep it to yourself, digesting or assimilating it as best you can" [K].    54 *learn of noble men* Brutus means that it will afford him pleasure to hear of the existence of good soldiers and noble men; he implies that, up to the present moment, Cassius has given no evidence of being either [K].    57 *If . . . not* whatever your insult was to me, I can bear it with equanimity, for I regard neither your boasts nor your anger [K].    59 *tempted* tested, provoked.

CASS.    Do not presume too much upon my love.
         I may do that I shall be sorry for.

BRU.     You have done that you should be sorry for.          65
         There is no terror, Cassius, in your threats;
         For I am arm'd so strong in honesty
         That they pass by me as the idle wind,
         Which I respect not. I did send to you
         For certain sums of gold, which you denied me;       70
         For I can raise no money by vile means.
         By heaven, I had rather coin my heart
         And drop my blood for drachmas than to wring
         From the hard hands of peasants their vile trash
         By any indirection. I did send                       75
         To you for gold to pay my legions,
         Which you denied me. Was that done like Cassius?
         Should I have answer'd Caius Cassius so?
         When Marcus Brutus grows so covetous
         To lock such rascal counters from his friends,       80
         Be ready, gods, with all your thunderbolts,
         Dash him to pieces!

CASS.                    I denied you not.

BRU.     You did.

CASS.    I did not. He was but a fool that brought
         My answer back. Brutus hath riv'd my heart.          85
         A friend should bear his friend's infirmities,
         But Brutus makes mine greater than they are.

BRU.     I do not, till you practise them on me.

CASS.    You love me not.

BRU.                     I do not like your faults.

---

67 *honesty* rectitude; consciousness of my own virtue [K]. 69 *respect* heed.    75
*indirection* irregular or unjust methods.    80 *such rascal counters* such wretched
dross. Counters were properly pieces of uncurrent coin employed by shopkeepers
and others to assist in "counting" or making computations; hence the word is
often used as a contemptuous term for "money" [K].    85 *riv'd* split.    96 *brav'd*
defied.    97 *Check'd* rebuked.    102 *Pluto's* F¹; some editors read "Plutus", but
Plutus, the Greek god of wealth and Pluto, god of the underworld, were usually

CASS.    A friendly eye could never see such faults.    90

BRU.    A flatterer's would not, though they do appear
As huge as high Olympus.

CASS.    Come, Antony, and young Octavius, come!
Revenge yourselves alone on Cassius.
For Cassius is aweary of the world:    95
Hated by one he loves; brav'd by his brother;
Check'd like a bondman; all his faults observ'd,
Set in a notebook, learn'd and conn'd by rote
To cast into my teeth. O, I could weep
My spirit from mine eyes! There is my dagger,    100
And here my naked breast; within, a heart
Dearer than Pluto's mine, richer than gold.
If that thou be'st a Roman, take it forth.
I, that denied thee gold, will give my heart.
Strike as thou didst at Cæsar; for I know,    105
When thou didst hate him worst, thou lov'dst him better
Than ever thou lov'dst Cassius.

BRU.                                    Sheathe your dagger.
Be angry when you will; it shall have scope.
Do what you will; dishonour shall be humour.
O Cassius, you are yoked with a lamb    110
That carries anger as the flint bears fire;
Who, much enforced, shows a hasty spark,
And straight is cold again.

CASS.                        Hath Cassius liv'd
To be but mirth and laughter to his Brutus
When grief and blood ill-temper'd vexeth him?    115

BRU.    When I spoke that, I was ill-temper'd too.

CASS.    Do you confess so much? Give me your hand.

---

considered as one by Renaissance writers. They had already been confused in
classical times.    104 *that denied* that, as you have claimed, denied.    108 *scope*
free play.    109 *dishonour . . . humour* any insults you offer me, I will excuse
as merely an effect of your irritable disposition [K].    112 *much enforced* sub-
jected to great provocation [K].    113 *straight* straightaway.    115 *blood ill-temper'd*
the humours of the body out of proper proportion, creating an unnatural disposition.

BRU.     And my heart too.

CASS.                        O Brutus!

BRU.                                  What's the matter?

CASS.    Have not you love enough to bear with me
         When that rash humour which my mother gave me        120
         Makes me forgetful?

BRU.                        Yes, Cassius; and from henceforth,
         When you are over-earnest with your Brutus,
         He'll think your mother chides, and leave you so.

                        *Enter a* Poet [*followed by* Lucilius,
                        Titinius, *and* Lucius].

POET.    Let me go in to see the generals!
         There is some grudge between 'em. 'Tis not meet        125
         They be alone.

LUCIL.   You shall not come to them.

POET.    Nothing but death shall stay me.

CASS.    How now? What's the matter?

POET.    For shame, you generals! What do you mean?             130
         Love and be friends, as two such men should be;
         For I have seen more years, I'm sure, than ye.

CASS.    Ha, ha! How vilely doth this cynic rhyme!

BRU.     Get you hence, sirrah! Saucy fellow, hence!

CASS.    Bear with him, Brutus. 'Tis his fashion.              135

BRU.     I'll know his humour when he knows his time.
         What should the wars do with these jigging fools?
         Companion, hence!

CASS.                        Away, away, be gone!    *Exit* Poet.

120 *rash humour* hasty temperament.    123 *your mother chides* it is merely your
inherited disposition that makes you speak irritably [K]. That Cassius inherited
his irritable temperament from his mother is Shakespeare's invention. *leave you
so* let it go at that.    136 *I'll know . . . time* I will admit his right to be eccen-
tric when he chooses a proper occasion to exhibit his eccentricity [K].    137 *jig-
ging* rhyming (a contemptuous term).    138 *Companion* fellow (in a contemptuous

BRU.    Lucilius and Titinius, bid the commanders
        Prepare to lodge their companies to-night.                    140

CASS.   And come yourselves, and bring Messala with you
        Immediately to us.        [*Exeunt* Lucilius *and* Titinius.]

BRU.                              Lucius, a bowl of wine. [*Exit* Lucius.]

CASS.   I did not think you could have been so angry.

BRU.    O Cassius, I am sick of many griefs.

CASS.   Of your philosophy you make no use                           145
        If you give place to accidental evils.

BRU.    No man bears sorrow better. Portia is dead.

CASS.   Ha! Portia?

BRU.    She is dead.

CASS.   How scap'd I killing when I cross'd you so?                   150
        O insupportable and touching loss!
        Upon what sickness?

BRU.                              Impatient of my absence,
        And grief that young Octavius with Mark Antony
        Have made themselves so strong; for with her death
        That tidings came. With this she fell distract,               155
        And (her attendants absent) swallow'd fire.

CASS.   And died so?

BRU.                  Even so.

CASS.                          O ye immortal gods!

                *Enter Boy* [Lucius], *with wine and
                tapers.*

BRU.    Speak no more of her. Give me a bowl of wine.
        In this I bury all unkindness, Cassius.            *Drinks.*

CASS.   My heart is thirsty for that noble pledge.                    160

---

sense).    145–6 *philosophy . . . evils* Brutus was a Stoic and as such his belief
was that nothing evil could happen to a good man. In other words, he held that
what Cassius calls "accidental evils" (misfortunes that come from the chances
of life) should be and are indifferent to the philosopher [K].    152 *Upon*
because of.    156 *swallow'd fire* This common but improbable story with regard
to Portia is found in Plutarch and other ancient writers [K].

Fill, Lucius, till the wine o'erswell the cup.
I cannot drink too much of Brutus' love.

                  [*Drinks. Exit* Lucius.]

         *Enter* Titinius *and* Messala.

BRU.    Come in, Titinius! Welcome, good Messala.
        Now sit we close about this taper here
        And call in question our necessities.          165

CASS.   Portia, art thou gone?

BRU.                No more, I pray you.
        Messala, I have here received letters
        That young Octavius and Mark Antony
        Come down upon us with a mighty power,
        Bending their expedition toward Philippi.     170

MES.   Myself have letters of the selfsame tenure.

BRU.    With what addition?

MES.   That by proscription and bills of outlawry
        Octavius, Antony, and Lepidus
        Have put to death an hundred senators.      175

BRU.    Therein our letters do not well agree.
        Mine speak of seventy senators that died
        By their proscriptions, Cicero being one.

CASS.   Cicero one?

MES.         Cicero is dead,
        And by that order of proscription.         180
        Had you your letters from your wife, my lord?

BRU.    No, Messala.

MES.   Nor nothing in your letters writ of her?

BRU.    Nothing, Messala.

MES.           That methinks is strange.

---

165 *call in question* examine, consider.   169 *power* army.   170 *Bending their expedition* directing their march with speed [K].   171 *tenure* tenour, purport. 181–92 *Had you . . . now* That this contradicts what Brutus had said of Portia's death in lines 147–56 has often been noted but never satisfactorily explained. It has been suggested that the scene had been revised and that the copy presented to the printer retained elements of both the original and the revised version.   192

| BRU. | Why ask you? Hear you aught of her in yours? | 185 |

MES.   No, my lord.

BRU.   Now as you are a Roman, tell me true.

MES.   Then like a Roman bear the truth I tell;
For certain she is dead, and by strange manner.

BRU.   Why, farewell, Portia. We must die, Messala.                185
With meditating that she must die once,
I have the patience to endure it now.

MES.   Even so great men great losses should endure.

CASS.  I have as much of this in art as you,
But yet my nature could not bear it so.                       195

BRU.   Well, to our work alive. What do you think
Of marching to Philippi presently?

CASS.  I do not think it good.

BRU.                          Your reason?

CASS.                                    This it is:
'Tis better that the enemy seek us.
So shall he waste his means, weary his soldiers,             200
Doing himself offence, whilst we, lying still,
Are full of rest, defence, and nimbleness.

BRU.   Good reasons must of force give place to better.
The people 'twixt Philippi and this ground
Do stand but in a forc'd affection;                           205
For they have grudg'd us contribution.
The enemy, marching along by them,
By them shall make a fuller number up,
Come on refresh'd, new-added, and encourag'd;
From which advantage shall we cut him off                     210
If at Philippi we do face him there,
These people at our back.

---

*patience* fortitude.    194 *art* theory.    196 *to our work alive* let us go about the
work which we, as living men, have to do [K].    197 *presently* at once.    201 *offence* harm.    203 *of force* perforce, of necessity.    205 *Do stand . . . affection*
are favourable to us, not heartily, but merely by compulsion [K].    209 *new-added*
reinforced.

CASS.                              Hear me, good brother.

BRU.    Under your pardon. You must note beside
That we have tried the utmost of our friends,
Our legions are brimful, our cause is ripe.                    215
The enemy increaseth every day;
We, at the height, are ready to decline.
There is a tide in the affairs of men
Which, taken at the flood, leads on to fortune;
Omitted, all the voyage of their life                         220
Is bound in shallows and in miseries.
On such a full sea are we now afloat,
And we must take the current when it serves
Or lose our ventures.

CASS.                              Then, with your will, go on.
We'll along ourselves and meet them at Philippi.             225

BRU.    The deep of night is crept upon our talk
And nature must obey necessity,
Which we will niggard with a little rest.
There is no more to say?

CASS.                              No more. Good night.
Early to-morrow will we rise and hence.                       230

BRU.    Lucius (*Enter* Lucius.) My gown. [*Exit* Lucius.] Fare-
well, good Messala.
Good night, Titinius. Noble, noble Cassius,
Good night and good repose!

CASS.                              O my dear brother,
This was an ill beginning of the night!
Never come such division 'tween our souls!                    235
Let it not, Brutus.

*Enter* Lucius, *with the gown.*

---

214 *tried . . . friends* already have all the support we can possibly expect from
our allies.    220 *Omitted* neglected, let slip.    221 *bound* confined.    224 *our
ventures* A figure from seafaring. The amount invested in a ship or cargo was
regularly spoken of as a man's "venture"; and persons who took risks of this kind
were called "adventurers" [K].    *with your will* as you desire.    228 *niggard* stint,
i.e. not sleep as much as we should.    231 *gown* dressing gown.    241 *knave*

BRU.                        Everything is well.

CASS.      Good night, my lord.

BRU.                              Good night, good brother.

TIT., MES. Good night, Lord Brutus.

BRU.                                   Farewell every one.

              *Exeunt* [Cassius, Titinius, *and* Mes-
              sala].

        Give me the gown. Where is thy instrument?

LUC.      Here in the tent.

BRU.                          What, thou speak'st drowsily?          240
          Poor knave, I blame thee not; thou art o'er-watch'd.
          Call Claudius and some other of my men;
          I'll have them sleep on cushions in my tent.

LUC.      Varro and Claudius!

              *Enter* Varro *and* Claudius.

VAR.      Calls my lord?                                             245

BRU.      I pray you, sirs, lie in my tent and sleep.
          It may be I shall raise you by-and-by
          On business to my brother Cassius.

VAR.      So please you, we will stand and watch your pleasure.

BRU.      I will not have it so. Lie down, good sirs.               250
          It may be I shall otherwise bethink me.
                          [Varro *and* Claudius *lie down.*]
          Look, Lucius, here's the book I sought for so;
          I put it in the pocket of my gown.

---

servant boy.  *o'er-watch'd* worn out by late hours, not sleeping.  242 *Claudius*
ROWE; F¹: "Claudio," and throughout scene.   247 *raise* rouse.   249 *watch your
pleasure* be attentive to any desires you may have.   250 *I will . . . so* The amia-
bility and humanity of Brutus towards his servants and subordinates is no less
striking than his dignified self-will with his equals [K].

| | |
|---|---|
| LUC. | I was sure your lordship did not give it me. |
| BRU. | Bear with me, good boy, I am much forgetful.                255 |
| | Canst thou hold up thy heavy eyes awhile, |
| | And touch thy instrument a strain or two? |
| LUC. | Ay, my lord, an't please you. |
| BRU. |                 It does, my boy. |
| | I trouble thee too much, but thou art willing. |
| LUC. | It is my duty, sir.                260 |
| BRU. | I should not urge thy duty past thy might. |
| | I know young bloods look for a time of rest. |
| LUC. | I have slept, my lord, already. |
| BRU. | It was well done; and thou shalt sleep again; |
| | I will not hold thee long. If I do live,                265 |
| | I will be good to thee. |

*Music, and a song.* [Lucius *falls asleep.*]

This is a sleepy tune. O murd'rous slumber!
Layest thou thy leaden mace upon my boy,
That plays thee music? Gentle knave, good night.
I will not do thee so much wrong to wake thee.                270
If thou dost nod, thou break'st thy instrument;
I'll take it from thee; and, good boy, good night.
Let me see, let me see. Is not the leaf turn'd down
Where I left reading? Here it is, I think.                [*Sits.*]

*Enter the* Ghost *of* Cæsar.

How ill this taper burns! Ha! who comes here?                275
I think it is the weakness of mine eyes
That shapes this monstrous apparition.
It comes upon me. Art thou anything?

---

261 *might* physical strength.    262 *young bloods* youthful constitutions.    267
*murd'rous* producing the appearance of death.    268 *mace* the staff carried by
a sheriff's officer with which he touches on the shoulder the person he arrests [ĸ].
275 *How ill . . . burns* It was a common belief that lights grow dim or "burn
blue" when a ghost or evil spirit is near [ĸ].    277 *monstrous* portentous, ominous.    278 *upon* against.    279 *Art thou . . . devil* This does not show that
Brutus fails to recognize the likeness of the apparition of Cæsar (a likeness which
would at once be clear to the audience), but merely that he is in doubt as to its

|         | Art thou some god, some angel, or some devil, |      |
|---------|-----------------------------------------------|------|
|         | That mak'st my blood cold and my hair to stare? | 280 |
|         | Speak to me what thou art. |      |
| GHOST.  | Thy evil spirit, Brutus. |      |
| BRU.    |                          Why com'st thou? |      |
| GHOST.  | To tell thee thou shalt see me at Philippi. |      |
| BRU.    | Well; then I shall see thee again? |      |
| GHOST.  | Ay, at Philippi. | 285 |
| BRU.    | Why, I will see thee at Philippi then.    [*Exit* Ghost.] |      |
|         | Now I have taken heart thou vanishest. |      |
|         | Ill spirit, I would hold more talk with thee. |      |
|         | Boy! Lucius! Varro! Claudius! Sirs! Awake! |      |
|         | Claudius! | 290 |
| LUC.    | The strings, my lord, are false. |      |
| BRU.    | He thinks he still is at his instrument. |      |
|         | Lucius, awake! |      |
| LUC.    | My lord? |      |
| BRU.    | Didst thou dream, Lucius, that thou so criedst out? | 295 |
| LUC.    | My lord, I do not know that I did cry. |      |
| BRU.    | Yes, that thou didst. Didst thou see anything? |      |
| LUC.    | Nothing, my lord. |      |
| BRU.    | Sleep again, Lucius. Sirrah Claudius! |      |
|         | [*To* Varro] Fellow thou, awake! | 300 |
| VAR.    | My lord? |      |
| CLAU.   | My lord? |      |
| BRU.    | Why did you so cry out, sirs, in your sleep? |      |

character. It was a common belief that spirits who were not ghosts might appear to one in the form of some departed friend or enemy [K].    280 *stare* stand on end.    287 *Now . . . vanishest* This line does not indicate that the vision is only subjective and therefore overcome by an exertion of Brutus's will, but merely that he tries to persuade himself that it is imaginary, as Macbeth attempts to do in the case of Banquo's ghost. The very next verse shows that he believes he has seen a spirit of some kind [K].    291 *false* discordant, out of tune.

BOTH.     Did we, my lord?

BRU.                         Ay. Saw you anything?

VAR.      No, my lord, I saw nothing.

CLAU.                              Nor I, my lord.                    305

BRU.      Go and commend me to my brother Cassius.
          Bid him set on his pow'rs betimes before,
          And we will follow.

BOTH.                         It shall be done, my lord.     *Exeunt*.

---

306 *commend me* convey my greetings.     307 *set on his pow'rs* advance his troops.

# Act Five

<hr>

[SCENE I. *Near Philippi.*]

*Enter* Octavius, Antony, *and their* Army.

OCT.  Now, Antony, our hopes are answered.
You said the enemy would not come down
But keep the hills and upper regions.
It proves not so. Their battles are at hand;
They mean to warn us at Philippi here,          5
Answering before we do demand of them.

ANT.  Tut! I am in their bosoms and I know
Wherefore they do it. They could be content
To visit other places, and come down
With fearful bravery, thinking by this face          10
To fasten in our thoughts that they have courage.
But 'tis not so.

*Enter a* Messenger.

MESS.                    Prepare you, generals.
The enemy comes on in gallant show;
Their bloody sign of battle is hung out,

<hr>

V.I. Between Act IV and Act V time enough has elapsed to enable the army of
Brutus and Cassius to march from Sardis in Lydia to Philippi in Macedonia. The
meeting at Sardis occurred, in historical fact, early in 42 B.C. and the Battle of
Philippi took place in the following autumn [K].  1 *answered* fulfilled.  4 *proves*
turns out to be.  *battles* armies.  5 *warn* challenge.  6 *Answering . . . them*
appearing in opposition to us before we have issued our challenge to them.  7
*in their bosoms* aware of their secret thoughts and intentions.  8–9 *could . . .
places* would prefer to be elsewhere.  10 *With fearful bravery* (a) in magnificent
array, but with timorous hearts [K] (b) with cowardly defiance.  *face* outward appearance.  14 *bloody sign of battle* the red flag ("vexillum") which, when hung out
at the general's tent, signified immediate attack [K].

|         | And something to be done immediately.                        | 15 |

ANT.    Octavius, lead your battle softly on
        Upon the left hand of the even field.

OCT.    Upon the right hand I. Keep thou the left.

ANT.    Why do you cross me in this exigent?

OCT.    I do not cross you; but I will do so.            *March.*   20

> *Drum. Enter* Brutus, Cassius, *and their*
> Army; [Lucilius, Titinius, Messala,
> *and others*].

BRU.    They stand and would have parley.

CASS.   Stand fast, Titinius. We must out and talk.

OCT.    Mark Antony, shall we give sign of battle?

ANT.    No, Cæsar, we will answer on their charge.
        Make forth. The generals would have some words.   25

OCT.    Stir not until the signal.

BRU.    Words before blows. Is it so, countrymen?

OCT.    Not that we love words better, as you do.

BRU.    Good words are better than bad strokes, Octavius.

ANT.    In your bad strokes, Brutus, you give good words;   30
        Witness the hole you made in Cæsar's heart,
        Crying "Long live! Hail, Cæsar!"

CASS.                              Antony,
        The posture of your blows are yet unknown;
        But for your words, they rob the Hybla bees,

---

16 *softly* slowly.    18 *Upon the right hand* Shakespeare shifts to the army of
Antony and Octavius what Plutarch reports as having occurred in that of Brutus
and Cassius, where Brutus insisted on commanding the right wing in spite of the
greater experience of Cassius. Shakespeare may have made the change to emphasize the power of Octavius over Antony.    19 *cross* oppose. *exigent* critical situa-
tion.    20 *I will do so* In this brief speech, Octavius asserts himself as the superior
of Antony in moral and intellectual force. We can, at the same time, recognize
that cold imperturbability which characterized the historical Augustus [K].    24
*we will . . . charge* we will meet their attack when they make it [K].    25 *Make
forth* step forward.    33 *posture . . . blows* kinds of blows that you will give.
34 *Hybla* a mountain (and a town) in Sicily, famous for honey. The honeyed

And leave them honeyless.

ANT.                                        Not stingless too.                    35

BRU.    O yes, and soundless too!
        For you have stol'n their buzzing, Antony,
        And very wisely threat before you sting.

ANT.    Villains! you did not so when your vile daggers
        Hack'd one another in the sides of Cæsar.              40
        You show'd your teeth like apes, and fawn'd like hounds,
        And bow'd like bondmen, kissing Cæsar's feet;
        Whilst damned Casca, like a cur, behind
        Struck Cæsar on the neck. O you flatterers!

CASS.   Flatterers? Now, Brutus, thank yourself!               45
        This tongue had not offended so to-day
        If Cassius might have rul'd.

OCT.    Come, come, the cause! If arguing make us sweat,
        The proof of it will turn to redder drops.
        Look,                                                  50
        I draw a sword against conspirators.
        When think you that the sword goes up again?
        Never, till Cæsar's three-and-thirty wounds
        Be well aveng'd, or till another Cæsar
        Have added slaughter to the sword of traitors.         55

BRU.    Cæsar, thou canst not die by traitors' hands
        Unless thou bring'st them with thee.

OCT.                                        So I hope.
        I was not born to die on Brutus' sword.

BRU.    O, if thou wert the noblest of thy strain,

words of Antony are his professions of friendship for the conspirators immediately
after the assassination of Cæsar [ᴋ].    39 *you did not so* you did not threaten or
give warning before you struck [ᴋ].    41 *like apes* in smiles like an ape's grin,
which one cannot trust, since he may mean to bite. Performing apes were common in Shakespeare's time and are often mentioned in the drama [ᴋ].    47 *rul'd*
had his way, in urging the death of Antony.    48 *cause* business at hand.    49
*proof* actual test.    54–5 *till another . . . traitors* till I too, another Cæsar, have
by my death at your hands stained your traitorous swords with further slaughter
[ᴋ].  56–7 *thou canst . . . with thee* A dignified way of disavowing the title of
"traitor" and casting it back at Octavius and Antony [ᴋ].    59 *strain* lineage,
family.

Young man, thou couldst not die more honourable.    60

CASS.  A peevish schoolboy, worthless of such honour,
Join'd with a masker and a reveller!

ANT.  Old Cassius still.

OCT.                     Come, Antony. Away!
Defiance, traitors, hurl we in your teeth.
If you dare fight to-day, come to the field;    65
If not, when you have stomachs.

                  *Exeunt* Octavius, Antony, *and* Army.

CASS.  Why, now blow wind, swell billow, and swim bark!
The storm is up, and all is on the hazard.

BRU.  Ho, Lucilius! Hark, a word with you.

                              Lucilius *stands forth.*

LUCIL.                    My lord?

              [Brutus *and* Lucilius *converse apart.*]

CASS.  Messala.                    Messala *stands forth.*

MES.          What says my general?

CASS.                    Messala,    70
This is my birthday; as this very day
Was Cassius born. Give me thy hand, Messala
Be thou my witness that against my will
(As Pompey was) am I compell'd to set
Upon one battle all our liberties.    75
You know that I held Epicurus strong
And his opinion. Now I change my mind
And partly credit things that do presage.
Coming from Sardis, on our former ensign

---

61 *peevish* childish.  *worthless* unworthy.   62 *masker* literally, one fond of en-
gaging in the half-dramatic social entertainment known as the "masque," which
was, in its beginning, a masquerade on a small scale, but which ultimately devel-
oped into a form of dramatic art [K].   66 *stomachs* appetites for battle.   68 *on
the hazard* at stake.   74 *As Pompey was* Before the Battle of Pharsalus Pompey
had in his camp many Roman nobles, who were clamorous for combat [K].  *set*
stake, hazard.   76 *I held Epicurus strong* I regarded Epicurus as right in his
views. Cassius refers to the Epicurean belief that the gods do not trouble themselves about human affairs, and that therefore to regard the signs and omens by
which the gods are thought to signify the future to men is a ridiculous supersti-
tion. As a matter of history, Cassius did profess the Epicurean philosophy [K].

Two mighty eagles fell; and there they perch'd,     80
Gorging and feeding from our soldiers' hands,
Who to Philippi here consorted us.
This morning are they fled away and gone,
And in their steads do ravens, crows, and kites
Fly o'er our heads and downward look on us     85
As we were sickly prey. Their shadows seem
A canopy most fatal, under which
Our army lies, ready to give up the ghost.

MES.     Believe not so.

CASS.                    I but believe it partly;
For I am fresh of spirit and resolv'd     90
To meet all perils very constantly.

BRU.     Even so, Lucilius.

CASS.                    Now, most noble Brutus,
The gods to-day stand friendly, that we may,
Lovers in peace, lead on our days to age!
But since the affairs of men rest still incertain,     95
Let's reason with the worst that may befall.
If we do lose this battle, then is this
The very last time we shall speak together.
What are you then determined to do?

BRU.     Even by the rule of that philosophy     100
By which I did blame Cato for the death
Which he did give himself — I know not how,
But I do find it cowardly and vile,
For fear of what might fall, so to prevent
The time of life — arming myself with patience     105
To stay the providence of some high powers

---

78 *presage* foretell events.   79 *former* forward.  *ensign* banner or standard.   80
*fell* swooped down.   84 *ravens . . . kites* regarded traditionally as birds of ill
omen.   86 *sickly prey* A condensed expression for "sick and likely to die and so
to become their prey" [K].   91 *constantly* resolutely.   95 *rest* remain (ROWE; F¹:
"rests").   *still* always.   96 *reason* reckon.   100–7 *Even by . . . below* I mean to
act according to the rule of that Stoic philosophy which made me blame Cato for
his suicide (somehow I find suicide cowardly) — that is, putting on the armour of
fortitude, I mean to await whatever the powers above have appointed [K].   101
*Cato* He killed himself (46 B.C.) to avoid falling into the hands of Cæsar, against
whom he had held out on the Pompeian side until the last [K].   106 *stay* await.

That govern us below.

CASS.                              Then, if we lose this battle,
You are contented to be led in triumph
Thorough the streets of Rome.

BRU.    No, Cassius, no. Think not, thou noble Roman,                110
That ever Brutus will go bound to Rome.
He bears too great a mind. But this same day
Must end that work the ides of March begun,
And whether we shall meet again I know not.
Therefore our everlasting farewell take.                            115
For ever and for ever farewell, Cassius!
If we do meet again, why, we shall smile;
If not, why then this parting was well made.

CASS.    For ever and for ever farewell, Brutus!
If we do meet again, we'll smile indeed;                            120
If not, 'tis true this parting was well made.

BRU.    Why then, lead on. O that a man might know
The end of this day's business ere it come!
But it sufficeth that the day will end,
And then the end is known. Come, ho! Away!    *Exeunt.* 125

❖❖❖❖❖❖❖❖❖❖❖❖❖❖❖

[SCENE II. *Near Philippi. The field of Battle.*]

*Alarum. Enter* Brutus *and* Messala.

BRU.    Ride, ride, Messala, ride, and give these bills
Unto the legions on the other side.       *Loud alarum.*
Let them set on at once; for I perceive
But cold demeanour in Octavius' wing,
And sudden push gives them the overthrow.
Ride, ride, Messala! Let them all come down.    *Exeunt.*

V.II.  1 *bills* written orders.    2 *other side* the flank commanded by Cassius.
4 *cold demeanour* lack of spirit or desire to fight.  *Octavius'* POPE; F¹: "Octavio's."
5 *push* assault.    6 *all come down* attack all at once.

◇◇◇◇◇◇◇◇◇◇◇◇◇◇◇◇◇

[SCENE III. *Another part of the field.*]

*Alarums. Enter* Cassius *and* Titinius.

CASS.  O, look, Titinius, look! The villains fly!
Myself have to mine own turn'd enemy.
This ensign here of mine was turning back;
I slew the coward and did take it from him.

TIT.  O Cassius, Brutus gave the word too early,    5
Who, having some advantage on Octavius,
Took it too eagerly. His soldiers fell to spoil,
Whilst we by Antony are all enclos'd.

*Enter* Pindarus.

PIN.  Fly further off, my lord! fly further off!
Mark Antony is in your tents, my lord.    10
Fly, therefore, noble Cassius, fly far off!

CASS.  This hill is far enough. Look, look, Titinius!
Are those my tents where I perceive the fire?

TIT.  They are, my lord.

CASS.                    Titinius, if thou lovest me,
Mount thou my horse and hide thy spurs in him    15
Till he have brought thee up to yonder troops
And here again, that I may rest assur'd
Whether yond troops are friend or enemy.

TIT.  I will be here again even with a thought.    *Exit.*

CASS.  Go, Pindarus, get higher on that hill.    20
My sight was ever thick. Regard Titinius,
And tell me what thou not'st about the field.
[Pindarus *goes up.*]

V.III. 1 *villains* his own men.    3 *ensign* standard-bearer.    4 *it* the standard.
11 *far* farther.    21 *thick* indistinct, dim.    *Regard* observe.

This day I breathed first. Time is come round,
And where I did begin, there shall I end.
My life is run his compass. Sirrah, what news?                    25

PIN.    (*above*) O my lord!

CASS.    What news?

PIN.    [*above*] Titinius is enclosed round about
With horsemen that make to him on the spur.
Yet he spurs on. Now they are almost on him.                     30
Now, Titinius!
Now some light. O, he lights too! He's ta'en. (*Shout.*)
    And hark!
They shout for joy.

CASS.                       Come down; behold no more.
O coward that I am to live so long
To see my best friend ta'en before my face!                      35

            *Enter* Pindarus [*from above*].

Come hither, sirrah.
In Parthia did I take thee prisoner;
And then I swore thee, saving of thy life,
That whatsoever I did bid thee do,
Thou shouldst attempt it. Come now, keep thine oath.             40
Now be a freeman, and with this good sword,
That ran through Cæsar's bowels, search this bosom.
Stand not to answer. Here, take thou the hilts;
And when my face is cover'd, as 'tis now,
Guide thou the sword. [Pindarus *stabs him*.] — Cæsar,
    thou art reveng'd                                            45
Even with the sword that kill'd thee.            [*Dies.*]

PIN.    So, I am free; yet would not so have been,
Durst I have done my will. O Cassius!

---

25 *compass* circuit, complete course.    29 *make to* approach.    32 *light* alight.
38 *swore thee* made thee swear.  *saving of* sparing.    42 *search* penetrate.    43 *the
hilts* Common in the plural, since the hilt of a sword consists of various parts [K].
47 *would not so have been* should not have chosen freedom on such conditions [K].
51 *change* exchange (of fortune).    52 *power* army.    54 *comfort* hearten, encour-
age.    65 *Mistrust of my success* fear that I would not succeed in my mission.

Far from this country Pindarus shall run,
Where never Roman shall take note of him.        *[Exit.]*  50

*Enter* Titinius *and* Messala.

MES.    It is but change, Titinius; for Octavius
Is overthrown by noble Brutus' power,
As Cassius' legions are by Antony.

TIT.    These tidings will well comfort Cassius.

MES.    Where did you leave him?

TIT.                                    All disconsolate,        55
With Pindarus his bondman, on this hill.

MES.    Is not that he that lies upon the ground?

TIT.    He lies not like the living. O my heart!

MES.    Is not that he?

TIT.                        No, this was he, Messala,
But Cassius is no more. O setting sun,        60
As in thy red rays thou dost sink to night,
So in his red blood Cassius' day is set!
The sun of Rome is set. Our day is gone;
Clouds, dews, and dangers come; our deeds are done!
Mistrust of my success hath done this deed.        65

MES.    Mistrust of good success hath done this deed.
O hateful Error, Melancholy's child,
Why dost thou show to the apt thoughts of men
The things that are not? O Error, soon conceiv'd,
Thou never com'st unto a happy birth,        70
But kill'st the mother that engend'red thee!

TIT.    What, Pindarus! Where art thou, Pindarus?

MES.    Seek him, Titinius, whilst I go to meet

---

68 *apt* ready (in this case, ready to entertain error) [K].    71 *kill'st the mother* as
vipers were supposed to do. The mother of "Error" is "Melancholy," and the
error destroys the mind that conceives it; for it leads to the death or downfall of
the person in question. Not a general truth, but general enough for Messala's
mood of despair [K].

The noble Brutus, thrusting this report
Into his ears. I may say "thrusting" it;                                    75
For piercing steel and darts envenomed
Shall be as welcome to the ears of Brutus
As tidings of this sight.

TIT.                                        Hie you, Messala,
And I will seek for Pindarus the while.    [*Exit* Messala.]
Why didst thou send me forth, brave Cassius?                                80
Did I not meet thy friends, and did not they
Put on my brows this wreath of victory
And bid me give it thee? Didst thou not hear their
shouts?
Alas, thou hast misconstrued everything!
But hold thee, take this garland on thy brow.                              85
Thy Brutus bid me give it thee, and I
Will do his bidding. Brutus, come apace
And see how I regarded Caius Cassius.
By your leave, gods. This is a Roman's part.
Come, Cassius' sword, and find Titinius' heart.    *Dies.*  90

Alarum. Enter Brutus, Messala, Young
Cato, Strato, Volumnius, and Lucilius.

BRU.    Where, where, Messala, doth his body lie?

MES.    Lo, yonder, and Titinius mourning it.

BRU.    Titinius' face is upward.

CATO.                              He is slain.

BRU.    O Julius Cæsar, thou art mighty yet!
Thy spirit walks abroad and turns our swords                               95
In our own proper entrails.                *Low alarums.*

CATO.                        Brave Titinius!

---

80 *brave* noble.    89 *By your leave* Titinius asks the permission of the gods to kill
himself before the time which they have appointed [K].    94 *O Julius . . . yet*
The significance of this speech in determining the central motive of the play has
been recognized by the best critics. The last two acts are closely bound to the
first three by this conception [K].    96 *In* into.  *proper* own.    97 *whe'r* whether
(F¹: "where").    101 *moe* more.    104 *Thasos* an island off the coast of Thrace, not
far from Philippi. Plutarch records that Brutus sent the body of Cassius thither

Look whe'r he have not crown'd dead Cassius.

BRU.     Are yet two Romans living such as these?
The last of all the Romans, fare thee well!
It is impossible that ever Rome                          100
Should breed thy fellow. Friends, I owe moe tears
To this dead man than you shall see me pay.
I shall find time, Cassius; I shall find time.
Come therefore, and to Thasos send his body.
His funerals shall not be in our camp,                   105
Lest it discomfort us. Lucilius, come;
And come, young Cato. Let us to the field.
Labeo and Flavius set our battles on.
'Tis three o'clock; and, Romans, yet ere night
We shall try fortune in a second fight.       *Exeunt.* 110


◇◇◇◇◇◇◇◇◇◇◇◇◇◇◇◇◇◇◇


[SCENE IV. *Another part of the field.*]

*Alarum. Enter* Brutus, Messala, [Young] Cato, Lucilius,
    *and* Flavius.

BRU.     Yet, countrymen, O, yet hold up your heads!

CATO.    What bastard doth not? Who will go with me?
I will proclaim my name about the field.
I am the son of Marcus Cato, ho!
A foe to tyrants, and my country's friend.                5
I am the son of Marcus Cato, ho!

*Enter* Soldiers *and fight.*

"fearing least his funerals within the campe should cause great disorder" [κ].
106 *discomfort us* discourage our soldiers.    108 *Flavius* F²; F¹: "Flavio."    110
*second fight* The "second fight" at Philippi really took place twenty days after
the first; but Shakespeare, as usual, has condensed the time for dramatic effect.
    V.IV. 2 *What bastard doth not* who is of such base blood, not being the true
son of a Roman, that he does not.

BRU.    And I am Brutus, Marcus Brutus I!
        Brutus, my country's friend! Know me for Brutus!

                                                    [*Exit.*]

                                        [Young Cato *falls.*]

LUCIL.  O young and noble Cato, art thou down?
        Why, now thou diest as bravely as Titinius,                    10
        And mayst be honour'd, being Cato's son.

1. SOLD. Yield, or thou diest.

LUCIL.                  Only I yield to die.
        [*Offers money.*] There is so much that thou wilt kill me
            straight.
        Kill Brutus, and be honour'd in his death.

1. SOLD. We must not. A noble prisoner!                               15

                        *Enter* Antony.

2. SOLD. Room ho! Tell Antony Brutus is ta'en.

1. SOLD. I'll tell the news. Here comes the general.
        Brutus is ta'en! Brutus is ta'en, my lord!

ANT.    Where is he?

LUCIL.  Safe, Antony; Brutus is safe enough.                         20
        I dare assure thee that no enemy
        Shall ever take alive the noble Brutus.
        The gods defend him from so great a shame!
        When you do find him, or alive or dead,
        He will be found like Brutus, like himself.                  25

ANT.    This is not Brutus, friend; but, I assure you,
        A prize no less in worth. Keep this man safe;
        Give him all kindness. I had rather have
        Such men my friends than enemies. Go on,
        And see whe'r Brutus be alive or dead;                       30

---

7–8 *And I . . . Brutus* Most editors assign these lines to Brutus although there is
no speech heading in F¹. Some have assigned them to Lucilius on the grounds that
he is here impersonating Brutus as Plutarch suggests that he did. These editors
argue that the speech heading at line 9 was simply misplaced in F¹.    10 *bravely*
nobly.    11 *mayst . . . son* mayest receive the honour which Cato's son should de-

And bring us word unto Octavius' tent
How every thing is chanc'd.                    *Exeunt.*

◇◇◇◇◇◇◇◇◇◇◇◇◇◇◇◇

[SCENE V. *Another part of the field.*]

*Enter* Brutus, Dardanius, Clitus, Strato, *and* Volumnius.

BRU.    Come, poor remains of friends, rest on this rock.

CLI.    Statilius show'd the torchlight; but, my lord,
He came not back. He is or ta'en or slain.

BRU.    Sit thee down, Clitus. Slaying is the word.
It is a deed in fashion. Hark thee, Clitus.    [*Whispers.*]    5

CLI.    What, I, my lord? No, not for all the world!

BRU.    Peace then. No words.

CLI.                        I'll rather kill myself.

BRU.    Hark thee, Dardanius.                [*Whispers.*]

DAR.                        Shall I do such a deed?

CLI.    O Dardanius!

DAR.    O Clitus!                                        10

CLI.    What ill request did Brutus make to thee?

DAR.    To kill him, Clitus. Look, he meditates.

CLI.    Now is that noble vessel full of grief,
That it runs over even at his eyes.

BRU.    Come hither, good Volumnius. List a word.        15

VOL.    What says my lord?

BRU.                        Why this, Volumnius.

---

serve and of which thou hast proved thyself worthy [K].    17 *the news* POPE; F¹:
"thee news."    30 *whe'r* whether (F¹: "where").

V.v. 1 *poor remains* pitiful survivors.    5 *deed in fashion* the suicides of Cassius and Titinius.

The ghost of Cæsar hath appear'd to me
Two several times by night — at Sardis once,
And this last night here in Philippi fields.
I know my hour is come.

VOL.                        Not so, my lord.                    20

BRU.    Nay, I am sure it is, Volumnius.
Thou seest the world, Volumnius, how it goes.
Our enemies have beat us to the pit.        *Low alarums.*
It is more worthy to leap in ourselves
Than tarry till they push us. Good Volumnius,           25
Thou know'st that we two went to school together.
Even for that our love of old, I prithee
Hold thou my sword-hilts whilst I run on it.

VOL.    That's not an office for a friend, my lord.    *Alarum still.*

CLI.    Fly, fly, my lord! There is no tarrying here.         30

BRU.    Farewell to you; and you; and you, Volumnius.
Strato, thou hast been all this while asleep.
Farewell to thee too, Strato. Countrymen,
My heart doth joy that yet in all my life
I found no man but he was true to me.                  35
I shall have glory by this losing day
More than Octavius and Mark Antony
By this vile conquest shall attain unto.
So fare you well at once; for Brutus' tongue
Hath almost ended his life's history.                  40
Night hangs upon mine eyes; my bones would rest,
That have but labour'd to attain this hour.

                    *Alarum. Cry within:* Fly, fly, fly!

CLI.    Fly, my lord, fly!

BRU.                        Hence! I will follow.

---

23 *pit* (a) trap such as that into which wild animals are driven, (b) grave, (c) abyss
of destruction.    38 *vile conquest* In the eyes of Brutus, the victory of Octavius
and Antony is the final downfall of Roman freedom. Not for a moment does he
doubt the justice of his own cause or the nobility of his action in killing Caesar
[K].    42 *this hour* the hour of rest and death. Death is no calamity according to
the Stoic belief of Brutus, but, if nobly attained, a rest from the evils of life [K].

[*Exeunt* Clitus, Dardanius, *and* Volumnius.]

I prithee, Strato, stay thou by thy lord.
Thou art a fellow of a good respect;                          45
Thy life hath had some smatch of honour in it.
Hold then my sword, and turn away thy face
While I do run upon it. Wilt thou, Strato?

STRA.    Give me your hand first. Fare you well, my lord.

BRU.     Farewell, good Strato. Cæsar, now be still.          50
I kill'd not thee with half so good a will.
                    [*He runs on his sword and*] *dies.*

                    *Alarum. Retreat. Enter* Octavius, An-
                    tony, Messala, Lucilius, *and the* Army.

OCT.     What man is that?

MES.     My master's man. Strato, where is thy master?

STRA.    Free from the bondage you are in, Messala.
The conquerors can but make a fire of him;                    55
For Brutus only overcame himself,
And no man else hath honour by his death.

LUCIL.   So Brutus should be found. I thank thee, Brutus,
That thou hast prov'd Lucilius' saying true.

OCT.     All that serv'd Brutus, I will entertain them.       60
Fellow, wilt thou bestow thy time with me?

STRA.    Ay, if Messala will prefer me to you.

OCT.     Do so, good Messala.

MES.     How died my master, Strato?

STRA.    I held the sword, and he did run on it.              65

MES.     Octavius, then take him to follow thee,

---

45 *respect* reputation.    46 *smatch* smack, relish or taste.    50 *Cæsar, now be still*
rest, perturbed spirit; for thou art avenged by this sacrifice which I make of myself. It was a common belief that the spirits of the dead were restless if unavenged
[K].    55 *can but . . . of him* can merely burn his body, never take him alive.
60 *entertain them* take them into my service.    61 *bestow* employ.    62 *prefer*
recommend.

That did the latest service to my master.

ANT.    This was the noblest Roman of them all.
All the conspirators save only he
Did that they did in envy of great Cæsar;                    70
He, only in a general honest thought
And common good to all, made one of them.
His life was gentle, and the elements
So mix'd in him that Nature might stand up
And say to all the world, "This was a man!"                  75

OCT.    According to his virtue let us use him,
With all respect and rites of burial.
Within my tent his bones to-night shall lie,
Most like a soldier, ordered honourably.
So call the field to rest, and let's away                    80
To part the glories of this happy day.

                                    [*Exeunt omnes.*]

---

67 *the latest service* By this touch we are assured of the essential nobility of
Strato's act in the opinion of his contemporaries [K].    68–79 *This was . . . ordered honourably* A valediction emphasizing what Shakespeare has taken pains to
keep before the audience from the outset — the patriotism of Brutus as contrasted
with the mixed motives of the other assassins [K].    71–2 *in a general . . . to all*
with a universally honourable purpose (unmixed with selfish considerations), and
for the sake of the good of all the Romans in common [K].    79 *ordered honourably* treated with all due honour [K].